making
Scale Models

making Scale Models

MARK FRIEND

THE CROWOOD PRESS

First published in 2014 by
The Crowood Press Ltd
Ramsbury, Marlborough
Wiltshire SN8 2HR
www.crowood.com

© Mark Friend 2014

All rights reserved. No part of this publication may be reproduced or transmitted in any form or by any means, electronic or mechanical, including photocopy, recording, or any information storage and retrieval system, without permission in writing from the publishers.
British Library Cataloguing-in-Publication Data
A catalogue record for this book is available from the British Library.
ISBN 978 1 84797 770 0

DEDICATION

For my parents, June and Terry who let me go to art school, George for 'helping' me with the models and Helen for living with them.

ACKNOWLEDGEMENTS

The author would like to thank Robert Youngson for taking the photographs, Mary Roscoe and Jones, Jones, Jones and Jones Ltd. for the use of studio space at Pollard Row, London.

Photographs: Robert Youngson

OXFORDSHIRE LIBRARY SERVICE	
3303195739	
Askews & Holts	03-Mar-2016
745.5928	£9.99

Typeset by Kelly-Anne Levey
Printed and bound in India by Replika Press Pvt Ltd

CONTENTS

INTRODUCTION		**7**
1	**TOOLS AND MATERIALS**	**9**
2	**SCALE**	**25**
3	**PROJECT: MAKING SIMPLE FORMS**	**29**
4	**PROJECT: MORE COMPLEX FORMS**	**35**
5	**PROJECT: MAKING A MODEL CHAIR**	**45**
6	**PROJECT: MAKING AN ORGANIC FORM**	**51**
7	**PROJECT: A HUMAN FIGURE IN 1:25 SCALE**	**61**
8	**PROJECT: AN ARCHITECTURAL ENVIRONMENT**	**69**
SUPPLIERS OF MATERIALS		**77**
FURTHRE INFORMATION		**78**
INDEX		**79**

INTRODUCTION

This book is aimed at the beginner and for those who want to learn the key methods and materials used to create a variety of models and modelled forms. From here you will find you can develop your own methods or variants on the techniques featured.

The book contains a list of the tools and materials needed plus step-by-step guides to completing small projects. These range from constructing simple forms through to modelling an accurate scale-modelled figure and full-colour and textured, organic form and architectural environment. It is an essential guide for those who want to know the basic skills and knowledge needed to make neat, accurate and expressive models.

Models are made for a variety of reasons. A designer may want to develop their ideas in three-dimensional form to realize a large-scale project. For example, a stage set, architectural project or piece of sculpture. In this case the model is made to convey the look and feel of the real thing that has yet to be created: the model as tool.

Alternatively a model may be an object in its own right. It can be figurative and descriptive of a recognizable environment. Some examples include a doll's house or model railway landscape, complete with furniture, trees and so on. Or it can be closer to a small piece of sculpture, as 'realistic' or as abstract as you want. This is where the idea of craft merges with art. It is up to you where you take the techniques you are about to learn.

OPPOSITE PAGE: **First steps: cutting a straight line.**

CHAPTER ONE

TOOLS AND MATERIALS

TOOLS

Blades

Let's begin with the basics. You will need a sharp blade, a straight edge to cut against, a means of measuring and a way of describing curves and circles. The easiest way to cut through a variety of materials is to use a scalpel handle that takes a size 10a blade, commonly known as a surgical blade or Swann-Morton®. There are two types of handle, a plain metal one and a plastic-coated one. Both are lightweight and very flexible. As you become more practised you will find that you draw rather than cut and these are the best tools for the job. The plastic-coated one is a little thicker but it can be easier on the hand, especially if you work for several hours. Though a conventional craft or Stanley knife is a useful tool, do not be tempted to use it as a substitute for a scalpel handle and blade; it is too heavy duty and you will never achieve the lightness of touch that is needed for fine, accurate cutting. The same goes for those sliding, disposable blades that are often sold in discount shops. Both of these are useful but the 10a should be the model maker's first choice.

The Swann-Morton® handle will also take a variety of other types of blades of varying length and shape; there is a particular curved blade used for creating lino-prints. These handles were originally designed for surgeons, whose work is not that dissimilar to a skilled model maker!

Saws

While a junior hacksaw is really designed for cutting metal you may find you use it for most larger cutting jobs. Modelling suppliers sell various other saws and jigs (jigs hold the material

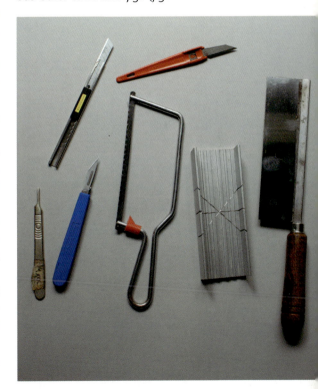

Scalpel handles, blades and saws.

OPPOSITE PAGE: Basic tools: always use a sharp blade.

to be cut and guide the blade). The other type of saw that you may find useful is a bead saw, which is a bit like a very fine hacksaw and is designed for fine woodwork.

Pliers

As with saws, there are all sizes of pliers but a small pair with a long, round 'nose' are the most useful. You can bend metal and wire as well as hold small materials or components steady while you glue or paint them. (Tweezers can be used for this too). A larger, heavier duty set of pliers is useful for cruder tasks and some include a blade for cutting wire and thin metal rod. However, you can get a pair exclusively for cutting.

Rulers and straight edges

You will need a metal ruler to cut a straight edge. A 12-inch/300mm ruler is a good flexible size but I recommend getting a 6-inch/150mm one for small work and a 1000mm or metre rule as well. You will need this for larger scale work, for instance, if you are constructing a foam board box to protect your model or to cut long strips of any sheet material.

There are a variety of manufacturers who make steel rules. Choose a rule that is not too heavy, but sturdy enough not to bend and slip. Some come with a thin, cork layer on the bottom edge to help grip, although this does mean it is slightly raised and this may cause you to cut an irregular line. My Heath Robinson tip is to get a flat steel rule and stick a piece of masking tape on the side that you are least likely to use for measuring (preferably the side with imperial measurements as from now I will use only the metric system). The tape causes enough friction to stop the rule sliding around, particularly if you are cutting a shiny sheet material, such as clear acetate or mirrored plastic. Just renew the tape from time to time. Use lighter fuel or a commercial product such as Clean Art to get rid of any gluey layers.

In addition, a flat, clear, plastic ruler with a grid printed on it can help with accurate positioning and right angles, though you shouldn't rely on this exclusively. The essential tool for this is discussed next.

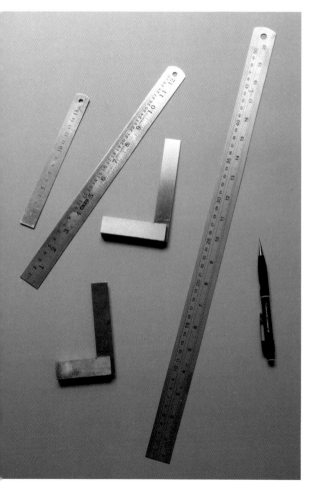

Steel rules, try squares and a click pencil for accuracy.

Metal squares

As with rulers it is possible to get a variety of sizes of square (or 'try square' to use its full title) for the accurate cutting of a 90-degree angle. While a conventional, woodworker's square with a wooden handle is useful; once again the model maker needs something a little more sophisticated. A small, metal square is best. Not only will it help ensure that you cut perfect 90-degree angles but it will also come in useful to check that any verticals are also correct, for instance, a series of square columns or uprights in an architectural model or the sides of a cuboid. You may need to check the internal angles when constructing a frame and you can even use it as a temporary support in a theatre model. For example, you may want to experiment with positions of walls or 'free-standing' surfaces in a modelled space.

Cutting mats

The correct cutting surface is as important as the correct blade. This means investing in a cutting mat. These consist of a rubber-like material that 'heals itself' when you have cut on it. They usually come in a variety of sizes and in some neutral shade that is restful to the eye. I am currently using a blue one with a white grid pattern on it, rather like graph paper. This can be useful for checking your right angles and whether that spare off-cut of card you are about to use is, in fact, square! I tend to carry an A4 cutting mat in my bag along with a scalpel and ruler, as well as my laptop! The mat ensures a non-slip working surface and prolongs the life of the blade. NEVER use a sheet of MDF, card or ply as a cutting surface. Your blade will be blunt in seconds and your work will suffer.

The right kind of pencil

While accuracy is ultimately achieved when cutting lines or shapes, it is essential that any marking out or measuring beforehand is also done with care. This means using a pencil that will give a consistent and clear mark. For this it is best to use a mechanical or 'click pencil' that takes a 0.5mm lead, rather than an ordinary pencil that needs sharpening regularly and may produce an irregular line. An HB lead is fine if used lightly. If you want something a little softer then use B grade but be careful not to press too hard as it will snap easily. Be careful also not to smudge the line. For very accurate drawing, H grade is good, but it can be difficult to see and it is tempting to press too hard and accidentally score the surface, if using card or wood sheets, such as obeche. This can be a problem if you've made a mistake and want to rub out the line.

Circles and curves

As well as straight lines, you will need to create circular shapes and curves. Pairs of compasses come with a blade attachment in place of the lead but I find them difficult to control. If the blade isn't of premium sharpness, it can snag. Far better I think, to draw the circle using a pair of compasses and then practise cutting a perfect circle. As well as achieving the end result of a disc, repetition of this method helps perfect all the techniques needed for good model making; lightness of touch, concentration and a flair for accuracy.

When it comes to creating ovals and other regular curves such as rounded corners, then arm yourself with as many geometrical tools as you wish. This isn't cheating! There are any number of templates and curves available. Especially useful are the ones for drawing small circles. Attempting to draw these with a pair of compasses can be very tricky. If you want to create a curve without geometry or mathematics but still need some help with drawing it free-hand, use a flexible curve. This is a bendy length of rubber-like material that has a metal core. It can hold any curved shape and you can draw along the line and cut it accordingly.

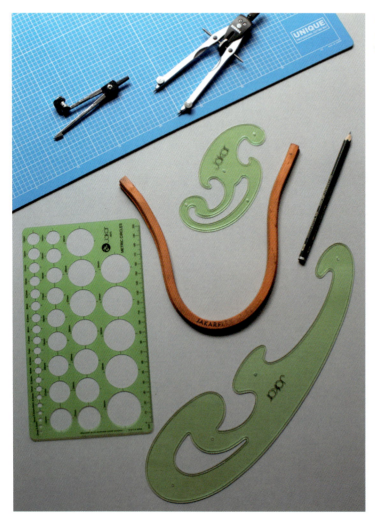

Curves and circles: templates, pairs of compasses and flexible curve.

Paintbrushes

There are innumerable types and sizes of paintbrush. The ones you need depend on the job but it is good to have a few very good quality brushes for fine work and any number of cheaper brushes for experimenting with, especially when creating different-textured surfaces. Eventually you may find that you will keep using the same, small number of your favourite brushes for a whole host of effects. It's surprising how many techniques and effects can be created using a small number of tools.

Here is a brief description of the most useful types of artist brush:

Round brush: has a pointed tip and is good for fine detail.

Flat brush: good for spreading paint evenly, for instance: paint and ink washes.

Fan brush: for spreading paint or ink over a larger surface, for instance, a planked stage made of strips of obeche.

Stippler: used to create texture by using a dabbing action.

Sometimes cheap brushes with hard bristles are better than more expensive ones, particularly if you are using any type of dry brushing technique to build up layers of colour or to

TOOLS AND MATERIALS

A variety of brushes to create different effects.

suggest grain. You can even use a small decorator's brush to texture larger areas or dust on colour over shapes and forms to give a light texture or soft focus effect. In fact, sometimes using cheaper brushes liberates your work as you feel less precious about damaging an inexpensive brush. A more general point to remember: almost anything can be a tool. The broad, scrubbing action of an old toothbrush might be just what is needed to distress a painted surface to reveal a texture or colour underneath. Never be afraid to experiment!

Files and sandpapers

Sandpapers come in all grades and each is suitable for a different task. Sometimes it is useful to mount the paper on a block of wood, particularly if you are sanding a larger, flat area. That way you exert an equal amount of pressure and avoid indentations from your fingertips. You could wrap a fine grade of sandpaper around a piece of tubing or pencil to finish off the edges of a circular hole. Sanding blocks, which can be re-used, particularly the finer grades, are also useful.

Most tool merchants and some art suppliers sell small files that are suitable for fine work with metal or plastic. Sandpaper nail files are a cross between the two, and although not designed for artwork, make a good artist's tool. More detailed descriptions of how to use these tools appear in the project chapters.

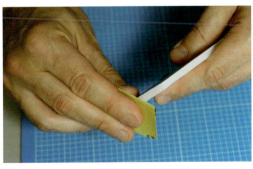

Using fine grade sandpaper to finish the edges.

MATERIALS

Card

There are two types of card that are the most useful and flexible; mount board and Bristol board. Mount board is suitable for a variety of rigid forms such as cuboids and boxes, as a base for floor and wall surfaces and as a laminate on foam board. It comes in pure white as well as black and white and a variety of other colours. Its conventional use is for creating the inner frame or mount for drawings and paintings in a picture frame. However it is also the perfect consistency for constructing the above forms. It is easy to cut with a scalpel blade and will take quite a bit of painting and texturing before it begins to warp, especially if it is securely mounted onto foam board or strengthened with a wooden frame or cross-piece supports. You can also glue or spray-mount coloured papers or images onto it. It is sometimes referred to as display board.

Bristol board is finer, rather like postcard. It also comes in many colours as well as white. While mount board can be made to curve by scoring lines on one side, Bristol board is best for finer and smaller curves. It soon becomes obvious which board is most suitable for the task. Bristol board is excellent for building up layers of fine detail when modelling architectural panelling.

There are other types of card that are either finer or heavier than the above, for example: stencil paper and heavy papers with textured surfaces and fine cards with grainy surfaces. There is also the thick, grey and rather fibrous card that you get on the back of sketchbooks. It can be bought separately as a sheet material. This is quite difficult to cut but it does provide a lovely rigid surface that is perfect for heavy mark-making and painting, as well as laminating.

The other most commonly used board is foam board. This comes in two distinct varieties and it is important to know the difference. Both can be used for constructing cuboids and boxes

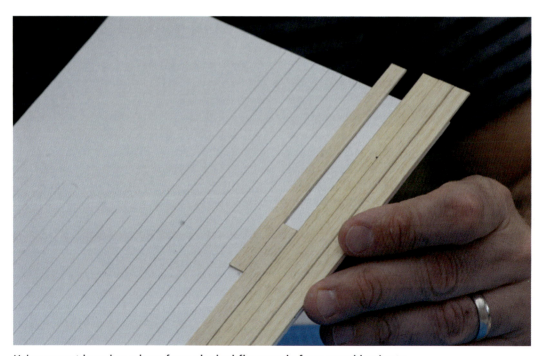

Using mount board as a base for a planked floor made from wood laminate.

and are most commonly used in architectural models and for making theatre model boxes. They come in sheets of black and white (and occasionally matt grey) and are sold in 3.5, 5 and 10mm thicknesses. They consist of a foam inner core, sandwiched between a tough paper (the white variety is slightly shiny). However there is a huge difference between cheap foam board and its more sophisticated cousin, Kapa board. This is because the inner foam core is made of an entirely different material and the tough paper either side can be easily peeled off. The foam core can also be sanded and carved to a high degree of finish, so this seemingly flat material can be worked to achieve surprisingly organic forms. Also Kapa board can adhere more easily and won't melt if you use a solvent-based glue. A colleague of mine once used foam board to create a landscape of hills and valleys, which he glued to an MDF base board using UHU® glue. By the time the model was to be viewed the next day, the UHU® had 'eaten' its way through the paper and dissolved every 'hill and dale' resulting in a very deflated landscape.

Pressed plastic sheeting.

Textured materials

As there are so many textured sheet materials available, I will just say a brief word about them. You need to look at them to decide what is exactly right for you. They come in the form of pressed papers and plastics, for example, brick patterns, as well as reproductions of architectural surfaces, such as metal tread plate and scored or planked designs. Some coloured, decorative papers also have texture as well as colour. Then there are tissue papers of varying weight and texture. The more formalized designs used to recreate, in specific scale, a certain surface are available from model-making suppliers. These are predominantly used by architectural model makers. Other more decorative or abstract designs are available from art shops and some specialist paper shops. They can be useful for recreating a wallpaper effect and can be painted to look like fabrics.

PLASTICS

By plastics, I mean the variety of pliable materials that can be used to create organic, free-form shape.

Clay, Plasticine and sculpture materials

Old fashioned, air-drying clay is suitable for only relatively crude forms or something that requires a quite rough, textured surface. Good old-fashioned Plasticine is familiar to most of us from childhood and can be sculpted into surprisingly detailed forms, though it will not harden of its own accord and will need a protective coating of PVA or thin Super Glue® to achieve any type of relative permanency. This can compromise the surface detail if used too liberally though.

There are several types of more sophisticated sculpting material, that will respond to a high level of detailing and can be hardened as well as 'brought back to life' for further detailing. Possibly the most well known brand is Super Sculpey®. Once it has been fashioned into shape it can be hardened by baking it in the oven. A heat gun can also be used on it at a moderate temperature.

Milliput® is something between the two. It is a little stickier than Super Sculpey®, closer in texture to Plasticine, though it can be hardened if exposed to heat. You will see how to make a scaled human figure using the first method mentioned, in the Project section.

WOOD

Nowadays wood is usually only used in model making as a laminate to create a visual effect or in fine mouldings to reproduce in scale, dado, picture rails and other architectural details and to create certain detailed aspects of furniture. It is rarely used as the main material for construction. In the past, many amateur enthusiasts began with matchstick models and graduated to creating extraordinary reproductions of the Tower of London or the Cutty Sark. This is a particularly niche area of model making and as this book is about using a wide variety of materials there isn't space to go into it further here.

Planking effects

Obeche is the best wood to use for reproducing a planked area, such as a theatre stage or domestic floorboards, or when making simple model wooden items such as old-fashioned crates. It comes in many thicknesses, from paper thin, which is good for laminating, through to thicker, self-supporting strips. It can be cut easily with a scalpel and will retain a fine line. It is also easily sanded and takes colour washes with paint or ink very effectively.

Balsa wood is softer and paler than obeche and is good for rough, weathered textures because it responds easily to scraping and rough scoring. Its smooth surface is quite fragile and it is easy to inflict unintentional marks and indentations as well. When working on a large area it is a good idea to protect it with some thick card.

A variety of wood laminate including obeche, balsa and walnut sheets.

Walnut also comes in sheets. It is darker than obeche with a consistency that makes it more likely to break along the grain. Bear in mind that its dark colour tends to dominate any paint or ink that you put on top of it.

Sometimes there is no substitute for the real thing (as in a planked floor) but often it is just as effective to recreate a wooden feel using Bristol board and inks, particularly if you are making fine carved furniture. It is a lot easier create the illusion of a fine Chippendale chair by cutting the fretwork out of Bristol board, than it would be to attempt this with wood. This is shown in the projects section of this book.

METALS

Rod, wire, mesh, metal sheets

Specialist model-making shops will supply brass and copper wire in a variety of thicknesses. It also comes in square and triangular sections as well as tubes. Cut the thinner rods using wire cutters and the medium sections (up to about 10mm) by scoring with a sharp blade, then snapping. Solid rods must be cut with a hacksaw. Piano wire is also useful. In its thicker form it can be very difficult to cut but the advantage is its incredible strength. Once bent it will retain the shape forever. Alternatively it will retain its straight line and is perfect for representing flown items in a theatre model as it resists even the clumsiest of butterfingers!

Along with solid metal sheets of copper, brass and aluminium, there are a variety of pressed metals and meshes available. Thin sheets are easy to cut with a blade, just score along a metal rule. Thicker sheets need to be scored and snapped. If you are attaching them to a card surface, use a combination of double-sided tape to 'locate' it and UHU® to stick it securely. The different glues and their uses are explained in the section below.

A variety of metals: brass and copper rod, piano wire and sheet metal and mesh.

Meshes can be used as a decorative surface or formed into sculptural shapes and covered with other materials.

PAINTS AND PRIMERS

There are three types of paint most useful to the model maker. These are gouaches, acrylics and aerosol spray paints.

The advantage of acrylics is that once they are dry, they are fixed. This means as well as being very durable, you can paint an acrylic wash over the top of each layer and build up colour and tone without the paints mixing. However some artists and designers dislike the plasticky feel of them. They also have a very slight sheen once they are dry. I admit to preferring gouaches.

Primers and paints: aerosol spray paints for a smooth finish. Tubes of gouache and acrylic.

(well-known brands include Marabu Buntlack and Humbrol) and the type sold in car accessory shops. These are much cheaper than the designers' paints but almost always have a gloss finish. Their colours are also limited to what is currently fashionable and available for cars.

Priming a model not only prepares the surface for the paint but also unifies the form by creating a skin. For priming, when using gouaches, use gesso, which is available ready mixed. A cheaper alternative is to mix white emulsion, thinned with water, with some PVA. You can then create your own textured primers by adding a little plaster or powdered filler. You can even add a little fine sand. Just experiment!

Specially formulated acrylic primers are available and aerosol paint primer is available in white as well as grey. A final word on paint: feel free to experiment using a combination of all the above. For example if you want an industrially produced surface that is showing signs of corrosion, you could spray the surface with a gloss paint, dull it down with a fine mist of designers' spray paint, then add a gouache and PVA wash. Alternatively you could create something of great beauty and depth by initially using gouaches then spraying over the top and then sponging it off. The combination of uses and effects are endless.

These are water-based, just like acrylics, but to my mind have a more natural feel. They are artists' paints. If you want to build up washes in the same way as acrylics, you can add a little PVA glue to fix the paint, although this will only work when it is thoroughly dry and will only take a very light wash. You could use a water-based matt varnish between washes.

I find gouaches best for dry brushing effects. When doing this, inevitably the colours do mix a little, but this builds up a variety of tones and marks that can create great depth.

Aerosol spray paints come in two types: the professional designers' range sold in art shops

INKS, STAINS AND VARNISHES

As well as the variety of paint effects, coloured inks can also be used to create a rich depth of colour and effects that range from the very controlled and sophisticated to the more free-form. As ever the rule is: experiment! However, one tip is to use ink to create a highlight of colour. For example, you may have sprayed or painted a piece of furniture made of card, such as a chair. A delicate application of ink with a very small brush, either along the edges or gently applied all over (perhaps on the upholstered seat, in a tone slightly lighter or darker than the base colour) will give the model more life. This technique can also be used along with wood stains and coloured varnishes, as well as over spray paints.

Obviously wood stains, as the name implies, are very good for staining modelled floor boards made from cut sheets of obeche or wood panelling, as well as mouldings and skirting. However if you prefer not to use wood, perhaps because it is easier to cut something very small out of card or Bristol board, such as the back of a Georgian dining chair, you can still apply wood stain. If you want to keep real sharpness to the model, you may not even have to prime the card as the wood stain will penetrate the card sufficiently. If the glue causes unevenness of tone, then apply a little primer all over and re-stain.

The most useful varnish for model making is spray varnish. It is available in gloss, satin and matt and because it is sprayed on, you can control the amount you apply and build up layers if necessary. As well as fixing a paint finish or creating a conventional, gloss finish, you can be an artist and not just a technician by, for example, experimenting over a larger surface area with varied layers, perhaps applying a dusting over the surface to manipulate the play of light to create movement and life.

GLUE

PVA/Wood glue

I love PVA! It is so versatile, strong and very clean to use. You can buy it from model-making suppliers who often sell a quick drying variety, though this isn't always an advantage, as part of the appeal of PVA is the flexibility it affords because it doesn't stick instantly. A cheaper way to buy it is by the gallon or litre from decora-

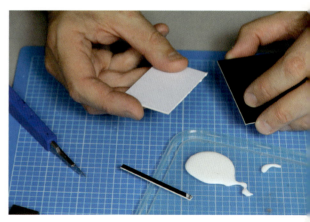

Using PVA glue to bond mount board.

tors' and builders' merchants. You can always decant some into a smaller bottle. Be sure that you use white PVA, which dries clear. Do not use carpenters' wood glue, which is specifically for wood and although sticks card adequately, it dries yellow. Do not be tempted to use washable PVA. It is really only useful for very young children to make art and craft. You will find it doesn't stick anything!

There are two main uses of PVA for the model maker. The first is to stick card to card, for example when making any type of boxy shape. You can apply the PVA along the edge of the card (mount board) then attach the edge carefully to the surface of the other piece of card. As the two pieces come together you will need to gently wipe away the excess with your finger. You can use the same method when sticking foam board edge to surface.

The second use for PVA is as a fixative. Mix it with gouaches or any water based paints to make them adhere more successfully to a surface. Don't mix it with acrylic paints. They don't go well together.

Use PVA to create textures by mixing it with plaster, sand, gravel, powders and so on. You can also use it rather like a varnish. It has its own particular look. Spray varnish is best for very fine work but giving something a PVA varnish may sometimes be called for. Try it and see what you think.

I apply PVA in a crude way when glueing. I dispense a little onto a spare piece of card and I use another bit of card, cut into a small strip about half a centimetre wide as a tiny spatula to scoop up the glue and run it along the edge of the card to be stuck. Some people use a cocktail stick or even a small brush. It's up to you to find your preferred tool.

You can also of course use PVA to stick wood to wood or wood to card or to seal a wooden structure.

Because it takes a while to go off, you may need to use masking tape or mini G-clamps to hold the card or wood together. Just make sure you have cleaned away any excess glue before applying the masking tape, otherwise you will stick the tape to the surface of the card and when you come to remove it, you will be left with glued tape on your nice, pristine model!

PVA is not suitable for glueing non-porous surfaces such as plastics. Read on to find out what is.

UHU® and tube contact adhesives

Not everyone gets on with UHU®. It can be difficult to control and does have its limitations. However, as with everything, if you know when to use it, it can be an excellent addition to your kit.

I would avoid using it as an alternative to PVA, as described above. It is difficult to clean away any excess and you can't apply it with a brush. It starts to go off quite quickly and once it does this it goes rubbery. It also has a tendency to 'string' and I have found the only way to avoid this is to adopt an elaborate arm movement, which involves pulling the tube of glue rapidly away from the material to be glued, once you have dispensed some from the tube.

UHU® is very good for gluing wooden supports to mount board, for instance, when framing out a piece of card to make it stronger. It is also good for applying wooden mouldings to card surfaces as well as laminating foam board with mount board. Use it with double-sided tape to ensure the surfaces stay together while drying.

UHU® can be used as a contact adhesive. This means it can stick some non-porous surfaces together. For example, it will stick plastic, textured sheeting to card. Apply the glue to both surfaces, then let it go off until it is semi-dry. Then bring the two surfaces together and they will stick almost instantly. Don't let it dry completely though as the two surfaces won't adhere to each other.

Super Glue® and accelerator

Yes, it is super in many ways but there are right and wrong ways to use Super Glue®. It is not the fix-all solution that many people think and should only be used to glue small items together. For example, you may be making a table with legs made from turned, wooden cocktail sticks. Super Glue® would be the right choice here as the surface area of the top of the cocktail stick is small.

When applying Super Glue® to wood, be aware that you may have to do it in two stages. The wood will most likely instantly absorb the glue so you must apply a second droplet and then bond the two surfaces together. This will also happen with card. Plastic will probably use less as it is not absorbent.

While you can buy Super Glue®, and variants of it, in newsagents and supermarkets, it is best to get it from a specialist model-maker's supplier. They will often stock three varieties. One is very runny and will stick immediately – particularly to your fingers! There is a thick, gel-like version that allows you to move the items before they stick altogether and there is the medium consistency, which I personally find the most useful. It is more controllable than the runny variety but goes off relatively quickly. However the runny variety, used with care, is a very useful glue.

TOOLS AND MATERIALS 21

Using Superglue as a hardener to strengthen a delicate model.

There is a product known as Zip Kicker or accelerator, which is a liquid, specially formulated to make glue set in an instant. You can either dispense a droplet onto the bonded items or it comes in a small spray bottle. It can be really useful when making something involving a lot of fiddly, repeat work. I once had to make a representation of an illuminated sign. The light bulbs were made of coloured beads. The letters were big so there were hundreds of them. I placed droplets of the middle consistency Super Glue® in lines, allowed it to go off slightly, then placed the beads with a pin. I did about ten at a time. I then added a droplet of the runny glue over the top of the bead and sprayed them with the accelerator. That way the beads became firmly fixed in place so if I brushed them with my hand when adding the next row, they didn't move.

The main disadvantage of using accelerator and indeed Super Glue® is that they both give off rather strong, poisonous fumes. Always open a window when Super glueing for any length of time and take breaks or you may find yourself feeling dizzy! Some plastics also have a chemical reaction to contact with Super Glue® and they will go misty. Test your materials first and if that is the case, use UHU®.

Spray mount, display mount and aerosol spray glues

These products were once principally used by graphic designers and exhibition designers in the days before computer-generated, printed graphics. They are still ubiquitous in art schools as their main use is in mounting drawings and presentational work.

Spray mount is a semi-permanent spray glue. This means you can peel the work away from the card or foam board and reposition it many times. It can also be used on plastic or metal sheeting though it won't adhere as firmly.

Display mount is probably of more use to the model maker as it is a permanent adhesive. It is ideal if you want to cover a large surface area of card or foam board with coloured or printed paper or even something you may have drawn or painted yourself. It has two advantages: the paper won't wrinkle as it would if you used a wet glue and it is very quick. There is a technique for applying it to the card or foam board and making sure that you stick it in the right place. When you apply a square or irregular shape that sits within a background mount (if it doesn't cover the whole surface) you can make small, locating marks to note where the top of the paper sits. If you get the top corners of the paper to be mounted in these positions then you know the rest of the paper will be stuck in the right place as you gently let it fall onto the surface of the card. As you do this, very gently smooth the paper in place to get rid of any bubbles. It is rather like wallpapering.

It is difficult to completely cover a large surface area with paper that is cut exactly to size. However careful you are, you will inevitably find that you overlap on one side and reveal some of the surface on the opposite side. Paper is an organic product and it does stretch. It is far easier to work with if your paper overlaps, by about a centimetre, the surface onto which it is being stuck. You can then trim off the excess using your metal ruler and very sharp scalpel blade.

Once you have stuck something down with display mount, you won't be able to remove it without it tearing and leaving some of the underside of the paper behind so be sure about what you are sticking when using this product! You may of course want to experiment with the effect I have just described to create that rough, collaged look when you see billboards with layer upon layer of old advertisements! As with everything I describe in this book, you will find your own way to expand and to create something different.

TAPE

There are many types of tape, Sellotape® is the one we all know. However, I don't really have a use for it when making models because there are more flexible and suitable alternatives. You can use it for its shiny appearance or apply it in a haphazard way to form a shiny, wrinkled surface.

Masking tape: practical uses

This is most commonly used by painters and decorators for masking areas that they don't want to get covered with paint, for example, the glass in a window frame. For the model maker it has another use: if you are constructing a box out of card or foam board or laminating card with obeche, masking tape will hold the pieces together while the glue dries. Because the nature of the adhesive on the tape is light, it is ideal for using on these delicate, papery surfaces. To make sure you don't damage the top surface of the card or board when removing the tape, here is a tip: before applying the tape, first tear or cut it to the required length. Then either stick it to

Using double-sided tape to create your own sticky-backed material.

your leg (if you are wearing trousers) and peel it off. This sounds a strange thing to do but this will 'dull' the adhesive and make it slightly less sticky. However it remains sticky enough to hold the card or board together. If you are wearing particularly expensive trousers (though I wouldn't advise this when model making!) or have bare legs, you can always run your finger over the sticky side of the tape for a similar effect. You will have to clean your hands after doing this for a while but the adhesive is quite harmless and washes off easily.

Masking tape: decorative uses

This tape can also be used to build up layers of fine detail when making furniture or working on architectural detail. If you are making a model table or chair and you want to create a turned leg, stick a length of tape to your cutting mat and then, using your metal rule and scalpel blade, cut a strip 1mm wide. Carefully peel it off the mat using the tip of the blade. You can then wrap it around a cocktail stick or piece of brass wire. The tape will probably stick to itself but you will need to fix it permanently before applying any paint or it will unravel. Do this using thin Super Glue®. The best way to do this is to put some glue onto a scrap piece of card, then apply a blob with a pin.

You can use these thin strips of tape to add detail around a door or window frame or to represent any slight raised or carved area. The Super Glue® will soak into the tape and once it is dry it can be primed and painted. Apply only as much glue as is needed and prime sparingly or you will lose the detail under too many layers. You can use this method in tandem with fine strips of plastic, available at specialist model-making suppliers.

Coloured tapes and electricians' LX tape

This can also be cut into thin strips and applied to any surface to create lines of colour. Reflective tape can be used in this way to represent recessed lighting in a floor or strips of neon light. Alternatively you can use it to create some sophisticated highlight colour.

Double-sided tape

This has a practical rather than decorative use. It is very strong and is best used when laminating mount board or any type of card or paper onto foam board and when glueing mount board with UHU®. Line it along the edges of the new layer if mounting thin card or paper and position it in the centre where the new layer may have a tendency to lift before the UHU® fully dries.

If you want to create model floorboards, apply double-sided tape to the whole underside of a sheet of obeche or walnut, before cutting them into strips. This will ensure that the wood is cut along your straight line and won't split along the grain. It is also a quick way to stick the floorboards down. Having removed the top, protective layer of the tape to stick it to the wood, peel back the bottom layer once you have cut the boards and stick them in place onto a mount board or foam board base. Occasionally one or two boards may lift up. Use a small amount of UHU® to secure them back in place.

You can use double-sided tape as an adhesive backing to virtually any sheet material, including decorative paper. If there is a particular part of a pattern on some printed paper, for example, a flower design, that you want to isolate and incorporate in your model, you can stick enough tape so that it goes beyond the image. Then carefully cut around the design and peel off the protective layer and stick the image on to the model. This is a quick, clean and strong way to stick smaller images, avoiding the use of wet glue or spray mount.

CHAPTER TWO

SCALE

Having looked at a variety of tools and materials, we now come to the area of model making that pulls all this practical knowledge together and makes your models read to scale.

A model that is not made to a consistent scale will not be convincing. It will look crude and won't sell the ideas behind it. An accurate scale model transforms the materials to make it a magical, microcosmic world in which the viewer is visually seduced and transported.

Theatre design models are a good example. These are rather like architectural models in that they communicate basic dimensional information along with the aesthetic ideas and intentions of the designer. However, as well as enabling the viewer to imagine how the real thing will look, they are objects of beauty in themselves. They are a way to realize all the creative ideas behind the design. An accurate scale model is a delightful object. A good grasp of scale will help achieve a convincing finished item.

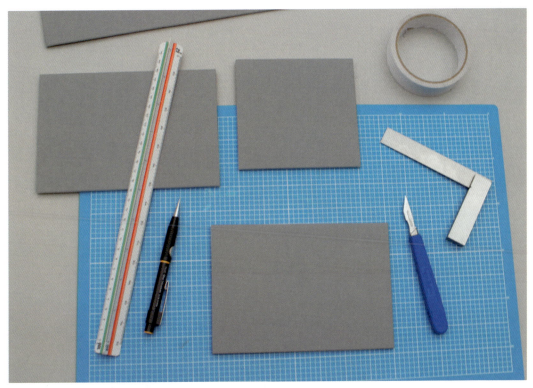

A scale ruler is an essential part of your kit.

THE SCALE RULER

Using the right scale

So how do we create accurate scale and what exactly does this mean? First, look at the most commonly used scales. For moels representing large areas, for exaple an architect's model of a riverside development that may incorporate several buildings, a landscaped area with trees, flowerbeds, roads, pathways and so on. For this a scale of 1:100 will most likely be used. This means that for every 1mm or 1cm on the model, there are 100 in real life. So an 1800mm human figure (a six-foot figure) is modelled at 18mm.

A scale of 1:50 is often used when developing ideas through the use of sketch models. This scale is big enough to explore ideas in more detail but small enough so that it doesn't take too much time to construct and assemble or use up too many expensive materials. 1:25 is about as small as you can go if you want to communicate the necessary detail that allows the viewer to really understand a design. There is something about this scale that allows the viewer to enter almost directly into the designer's world, to 'walk' into the model.

1:10 is really quite large and is not often used by designers but is best if the model is the end in itself. The level of detail and use of materials has to be very sophisticated as everything is magnified, for instance, the features on the face of a human figure, the texture on a brick wall, the paint work or fabric used on a piece of furniture. This scale is perhaps best suited to the sculptural maquette. This is a scale representation of either figurative or more abstract, sculptural forms.

The more you use the scale rule, the keener your sense of scale will become; this means you will develop a more sophisticated idea about which materials and textures are most appropriate to the item you are depicting. You may find yourself moving away from a naive style that would incorporate found materials, such as a toothpaste tube lid to represent a lampshade, into a more artful method where you would create the lampshade in miniature. As ever, it is up to you when and how you employ these techniques; when to retain a naive, ready-made charm and when to create work of great sophistication.

Drawing an accurately scaled-down human figure.

SCALE 27

The brickwork for this window has been carefully drawn to scale before the modeller uses a scalpel to cut out the window frame.

DEVELOPING A SENSE OF SCALE

If, for example, you wanted to create an oversized environment with an 'Alice in Wonderland' feel, it would be especially important to be clear about scale because you would be mixing the scales up – a 'real life' environment of objects and furniture combined with an oversized human figure. This means the application of colour to the skin and the choice of materials used to re-create the clothing would have to be a very particulate choice. Sometimes it is possible to use actual fabric in model-making, though more often than not, we choose to use other materials to represent the 'real thing'.

A clever trick for giving a modelled surface a soft feel, as if it were made of fabric, would be to use fabric itself to 'print' its texture. Say, for example, that you were making a model sofa or chair. In this instance, the cushions would most likely have been made from sculpted foam board or Plasticine. Once these surfaces had been lightly primed, you would then apply a base colour. Then you might get a piece of fine cotton or calico and apply a little gouache paint either in a lighter or in a darker tone than the base colour to the fabric surface, making sure the paint wasn't too watery. Then you would press the painted surface of the fabric to the model chair, and whe you removed the fabric, it would have left an imprint of the weave.

Alternatively, or even in addition to this technique, you could use a pin to prick the surface of the model very gently and create a kind of fabric-like texture. A method like this is all about tricking the eye and the play of light across a surface. This is not about using scale in a directly mathematical way, though of course it does relate to it, but about training your eye to develop an in-built sense of scale.

CHAPTER THREE

PROJECT:
Making Simple Forms

MAKING A REGULAR SHAPE

A cube

Let's begin with something that is both simple and complex! The result is a shape of beautiful simplicity that consists of a form with six sides that are exactly the same size and shape. However to achieve this there is a particular method that takes into account the type of material you are using and its thickness. While this relatively simple piece of construction is essentially a straightforward exercise, you will see that we use the same methods time and again when moving into more complex model-making projects.

Let's make a cube that is 5cm x 5cm x 5cm. Begin by marking out a strip onto some mount board that is 5cm by just over 30cm. This will be long enough to cut six 5cm facia. Use your try square and metal rule to mark out each facia, then cut them out using your scalpel and small metal rule. You will very quickly realize that if you place the pieces at right angles, edge to edge, they won't be the right size. This is because of the thickness of the card. This means you must trim the pieces appropriately to achieve the six equal facia that form the cube.

Select two facia as the 'sides'. Select another two facia to be the 'base' and 'top' and the last two to be the 'front' and 'back'. I have used inverted commas because, once the cube has been made, should you decide to paint it all one colour, the 'sides' will be indistinguishable from any other facia. The two 'sides' remain at 5cm x 5cm. The 'base' and 'top' will need to be trimmed by the thickness of the card along their two edges that meet the 'sides'.

The 'front' and 'back' will need to be trimmed along all four edges. The easiest way to trim the edges accurately is to place a piece of the material you are using, in this case the mount board, along each edge and mark it using your scalpel. Don't bother marking it with a pencil. While it

Making the simplest form: a cube.

OPPOSITE PAGE: Dividing up a strip to make a cube.

PROJECT: MAKING SIMPLE FORMS

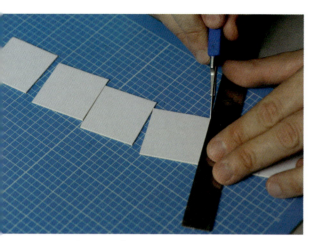

Cutting out the squares using a sharp blade and a small metal rule.

Trimming the edge to size to make the facia form a cube.

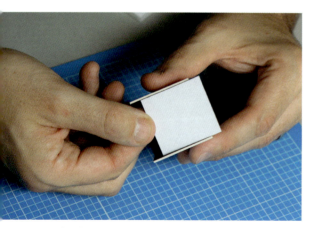

Checking that the sides all fit together.

is good to encourage accurate work with the pencil, using the scalpel directly eliminates, in this instance, an unnecessary extra stage that can introduce a margin of error. Where possible always use the scalpel to mark the beginning of where you want to make a cut. You can always join the points with a pencil line as a guide to where to place the ruler, but it is the scalpel marks that will really tell you this.

Once you have trimmed all the edges, begin construction by joining the base to the left side and the top to the right side. The top and base will sit within the sides.

Stick together by applying the PVA glue to the edge of the base and top. You can use a small brush to apply the glue, though my preferred method is to cut a sliver of card, and use it as an applicator dipping it into the glue. Use a little more glue than you need. Hold the edges together for a few seconds and allow the glue to be absorbed into the card and to go off slightly. Gently wipe away any excess with your finger. If you have judged it right, this minimal amount of glue will be virtually dry once you rub your fingers together and flick away the remains. Keep a tissue or cloth to hand if necessary. Because PVA doesn't dry instantly you can move the pieces if you haven't quite placed them correctly first time. Use your try square to check the right angle.

Once the edges have dried fully, add the front and back to the left side and base. If you think it necessary, cut or tear a small piece of masking tape to temporarily keep the facia in place. Remember to 'de-stick' the tape. The papery surface of the mount board will be delicate. You don't want to remove the top surface and spoil your pristine work. The same goes for foam board. Be careful too that all excess glue has been removed or the masking tape will be permanently stuck to the surface.

When these edges have been stuck together, it is time to complete the cube by adding the top and right sides.

PROJECT: MAKING SIMPLE FORMS

Carefully applying PVA glue with a small strip of card.

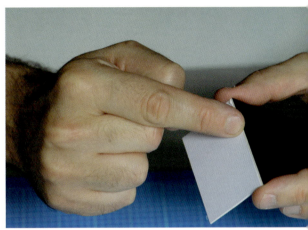

Removing excess glue.

Having made sure the whole thing is completely dry and secure, you can now take it to the next stage. Using very fine sandpaper, gently sand the edges of cube. Pay some attention to the joins. However accurately you have assembled the facia, there may be a slight 'seam' where the edges have been stuck together. Gently rub the sandpaper along the length of the join. You may also want to gently round off the corners of the cube. This will deal with any slip of the scalpel when cutting the facia out and also prevent the sharp corners from being crushed. You may think that this compromises the accuracy and sharpness of your work. It is up to you whether you want to do this or not but it is worth noting that the eye will read a slightly rounded edge and corner as a crisp point and line.

You may think that you could use UHU® or Super Glue® to construct the cube. It is possible. However, the liquid and organic nature of PVA makes the whole process cleaner and more flexible. In this instance UHU®, with its tendency to form stringy fronds, is not so easy to work with. If you attempt to remove any excess, the whole lot will most likely come away. In addition it does not respond very well to sanding.

Super Glue® should only really be used for spot glueing. This means sticking very small items together using a small amount of glue. The more

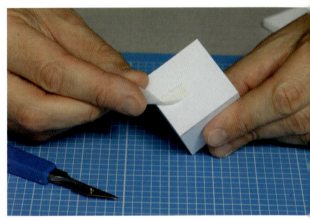

Using masking tape to keep the facia in place.

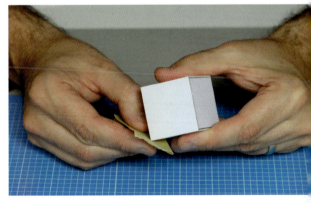

Gently sand along the seams and edges. You can round off the corners before priming.

PROJECT: MAKING SIMPLE FORMS

Applying a primer with a broad brush.

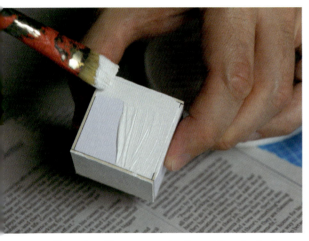
Covering the seams with broad brush strokes.

A stipple brush to create a textured surface.

Super Glue® you use, the more likely it is to get on your fingers! (Once PVA has dried it will sand very well.)

Once all the pieces are glued together, you should prime the surface before painting. Depending on the final result desired, there are several stages of surface preparation that you can employ.

For a completely seamless surface, which you can build up in layers, first coat the whole cube in a thin coat of PVA. Do this in stages, say two facia at a time; you don't want to get finger-marks in the glue or stick the cube to the table or cutting mat! Once all the facia are completely dry, lightly sand them. Now repeat the process using a mixture of very fine filler and PVA. Once again, very lightly sand the whole cube. Now use an aerosol primer to gently dust the surface with a layer. Again, do this in stages, allowing each layer to dry completely. Finally, use an aerosol paint to colour the cube. Obviously, if you don't want such a fine finish, then follow the less-complicated procedure below.

If you want the cube to have different colour facia, use some masking tape to mask the edges of each facia. Spray the lighter colours first; for example yellow before blue. This is because darker colours will overlay the lighter colours more easily.

For a less industrial but nonetheless sophisticated result, prime the surface of the whole cube using gesso. Once it is dry, gently sand the surface and either apply colour using aerosol paint or, using a soft brush, add colour with gouache. As it is water-based, try to apply the colour in one layer. The nature of gouache allows you to do this and achieve a solid surface. You may want to protect the surface by spraying it with matt varnish.

Alternatively you may want to create a textured surface. Pure gesso or white acrylic paint will respond to various brush techniques. A stiffer brush will leave directional brush marks. For an evenly textured effect, use a stipple brush.

You can experiment with this by adding varying amounts of filler or plaster and PVA to the gesso. You can also add some fine sand. Be sure to mix it thoroughly and make enough to complete the job. If you have to apply it in stages, take note of the recipe so that you end up with a consistent finish on all surfaces.

Depending on the nature of the textured surface you have chosen to create, you can apply colour in a variety of ways, building up contrasting layers or creating depth in one colour.

The cube in the picture has been primed with white acrylic. I used an old stiff brush to apply it and a stipple brush to create an evenly textured surface.

You can use a fan brush to create a colour wash that brings out the texture. Once the wash is dry, use a small, round-nosed brush to create a contrasting line pattern in the same or another colour.

The marking out, trimming and sticking tech-

Using a fan brush to create colour washes and bring out the texture.

niques used on this first project can be used when constructing any form that contains right angles. The next project involves taking it further to create irregular angles and shapes.

Creating contrasting brush work with different brushes.

| CHAPTER FOUR | 35 |

PROJECT:
More Complex Forms

MAKING AN IRREGULAR SHAPE

An exploding star

Begin as before by selecting the materials and marking out the design. This time you will be using three types of card: mount board for the main construction, Bristol board and metallic card for detail. You will also be creating your own metallic and textured effect using an everyday, household product. This project covers models that could be built or they could simply be constructed for fun.

Marking out

Mark out your design on paper first. You can use tracing paper to transfer it to the mount board. Cut a square piece of mount board that is big enough for your design rather than trying to work on a small area of a large sheet of mount board.

Cutting

This design involves pointed shapes; sets of two lines meet to form triangular points, which requires a particular way of cutting.

OPPOSITE PAGE: **A more complex, angular form.**

Always begin by placing the scalpel where the lines meet and cut away from that point. Doing it in reverse risks moving the scalpel too far along the line and cutting into the main body of the shape. Cutting away from the point means that you are completely in control. As with all cutting, lightly score a line with the blade first and go over it two or three times. You may want to use the metal rule for each cut, though once you are practised you may find that you can do the second or third stroke without the metal rule. This is because the initial cut has done the work for you and acts as a guide for the blade. You can always go back to the top of the point once you have made the long cuts. Make sure you can pull the now unwanted section of card away from the main shape without tearing it. You can trim any shreds of card left attached with the blade. For work like this it is as important as ever to have a sharp blade.

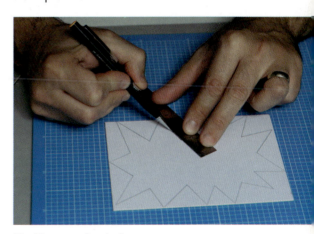

Marking out the design.

Cutting away from the corners

Working your way around the shape.

Giving the flat form a thickness.

Work your way around the star shape, pulling away the unwanted pieces. While it is preferable to keep a clear working space, don't get too obsessive. Do a mini clean-up after each task. It is fine to have a few odd pieces of card to hand, either as glue or paint palettes or as homemade tools for scraping away glue, mark-making and so on. The other extreme is when you find yourself working in a very small area surrounded by piles of card, tape and tools! This generally happens after several hours of intense work. Take time to clear your space and your head. Marcel Duchamp, the artist famous for his ready-made sculptures, said that you should clear out your studio at least twice in your lifetime!

Now that you have the main star shape, the next stage is to create the sections that will form the thick edge. You don't have to waste time measuring how long the strip has to be in total or indeed how long each section has to be for every point of the star. Make an educated guess and cut one or two long strips to the desired thickness. Don't worry about cutting a little more than you think you may need.

As each point will be formed by varying lengths of card, the next stage is to cut several smaller lengths from the long ones. Maybe use one short length then use it to mark the length of each point. It is often easier to use this method than to measure everything. A ruler won't always fit into little angles. Mark and cut a few short strips at a time. Again, make them a little longer than necessary because you are about to learn a new technique.

Chamfering

To create the sharp points of the star, you will need to chamfer the inner edge of the pieces that will form these points.

You may have seen the results of this technique when looking at a painting or drawing which is most likely surrounded by a mount, that is, mount board used for its conventional purpose. This inner frame will have sloped or chamfered edges. A picture framer may have used a special tool, which holds a very sharp blade at a forty-five-degree angle. Once you have cut out a window, it is run along the edge of the card to create this effect. If you want to get one of these, a specialist framer may provide one. However, this book shows you how to do it simply using a metal rule and scalpel. The advantage of this is that you can vary the angle of cutting. If the point of the star is quite acute, then you need an angle greater than forty-five degrees.

So here's how to do it. Place your metal rule about half a centimetre from the edge of the card. If you are right handed, hold the rule firmly in place with your left hand. Then with your right hand, using a sharp blade, place the blade on the top left edge of the piece of card. Angle the scalpel so that the top of the blade is resting against the edge of the metal rule and the tip of the blade is level with the top edge of the card. Now draw the scalpel across the top edge at a slow but regular pace until you reach the other side. Try and do this in one slow, controlled movement. Ensure that the angle of the blade is consistent. Once you have done this, hold the piece of card up to your eye and check your angle. It does take practice! The trick is not to worry about keeping the scalpel at the correct angle but to think about a smooth movement and visualize the perfect result as you are doing it.

To deal with any irregularity use a very fine piece of sandpaper to gently sand the chamfered edge along its length. Take care not to rub too hard or you will pull away the top surface of the card. Check that the angle is consistent along the edge of the card, that is, that the card in profile reaches a point.

Once you have done this, place the whole piece of card against the main star shape design. Having chamfered the end you can now determine the exact length that this section that forms

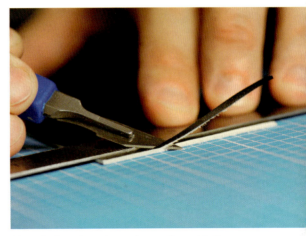

Chamfering the edge using a sharp blade.

Fitting the edges together.

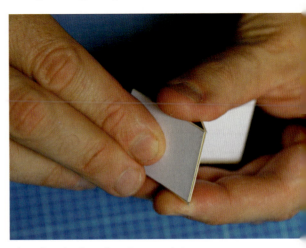

Chamfered edges forming a point.

The three-dimensional shape complete.

the edge needs to be. Using your try square cut it to size. Now stick it on using PVA glue as you did with the cube.

While it is drying, chamfer the end of the next piece. When this is done, hold it in place so that the two chamfered ends meet to form a very satisfying point. Mark the end of this piece and cut it to size. Now continue working your way around all the points, glueing each one as you go. Use small pieces of masking tape to keep them in place if you like.

Once you have created all the points of the star, remove all the pieces of masking tape.

A shape like this has the advantage of inherent strength because the sides of each point help support each other. However if you want to add extra strength, run a line of glue along the inner edges of the model. You can use more PVA by dispensing it from a small bottle with a pointed top dispenser or you could use UHU®, which will dry relatively quickly. For real quickness, you can use the very runny variety of Super Glue®, though be aware that this may bleed through the joins in the card. Only use this if you are planning to prime the whole model. You could also use medium consistency Super Glue® and you can always speed up the process by spraying it with glue accelerator.

If you think it necessary, now is the time to lightly sand any edges. It is most likely that you will want to leave the points as crisp as possible but sand along the seam where the main body of the star joins its thickness. As ever, always sand along the length of the join.

Making your own textured surface

This design involves a highly contrasting edge both in colour and texture. This is not a definitive technique but is an attempt to encourage you to think about combining materials and techniques to create your own methods and effects.

To create a textured, metallic surface, cut a strip of household tin foil. Make it slightly bigger than the edge that it will cover. Gently scrunch it up but don't form it into a tight ball. Slowly and carefully unfurl the foil taking care not to tear it. If this happens though don't worry because you are about to add double-sided tape to it.

Smooth out the foil so that it is flat but retains the criss-cross folds you have just created. You will find the strip of foil is now an irregular shape. This is one reason why we cut it larger than the surface onto which it will be attached.

Now unroll a length of double-sided tape and attach it to the dull side of the tin foil. You can make the length of tape run slightly over the foil strip onto your cutting mat. Then cut it with your scalpel.

If you find your cutting mat is getting a build-up of bits of tape or residue, use a metal rule to gently scrape it off and a product such as Clean Art or a little white spirit or lighter fuel to clean your mat. Then wipe over with a damp cloth.

Place your long metal rule along the length of the double-sided tape. You can place it along the exact edge of the tape or to guarantee a straight line, just below the edge so that when you run the blade along it, you cut into the tape as well as the foil. This also has the advantage of making sure the foil won't snag as it is surprisingly fragile especially if your blade isn't of premium sharpness.

Depending how big your piece of foil needs to be, you may need parallel strips of double-sided tape. Having cut one strip, place the next strip exactly edge to edge and cut to size in the same way.

You have now created your very own 'sticky-backed' product. Imagine how many of your own you can create using different textured

Adding a metallic edge.

Gently creating texture.

Flattening out the foil before applying double-sided tape.

PROJECT: MORE COMPLEX FORMS

Cutting to size with a sharp blade.

Applying aerosol spray paint

There is an art to successfully coating a surface with aerosol spray paint. The main thing to remember is to build it up in layers. You must of course make sure that you only use this product in a well-ventilated area. If you are lucky enough to have a studio space then a special spray booth with an extractor fan, is the best place to do this. However, on dry days it is perfectly fine to work outside. Beware of the wind changing direction and do wear a mask.

Before you begin, be aware that the spray will go well beyond the area in which you point the aerosol can. Place the model on some old newspaper. This is better than plastic as newspaper is more absorbent and in plentiful supply.

Hold the can at least thirty centimetres away from the surface to be sprayed and use light even strokes to dust the surface with colour. Once this is dry, add another layer and build up as you go. Never be tempted to rush this process! Always ensure each layer is thoroughly dry before applying the next.

It is possible to create a variety of shades and colours within one design by using several paint colours and to build up the layers in the same way. This is particularly effective if you want to create a subtle, metallic effect. Try spraying a surface with a metallic paint then covering it with a light layer of colour, allowing the metallic paint to partially show through. Then apply the metallic paint over the top and repeat the process as many times as you like. This simple technique is surprisingly controllable and you will be impressed with the sophisticated result. It can transform the most humdrum materials into something quite spectacular.

You can use a gloss spray paint, or for a subtler and more varied surface, use a matt spray paint and then add a layer of varnish. You can also combine very fine layers of matt varnish and semi-gloss varnish to create depth and variety of finish.

papers and fabrics. Think about tissue paper, sandpaper, or simple coloured paper. This is a very useful technique if you want to create thin strips of colour or a fine reflective edge. Before applying your reflective edging you need to apply the main texture and colour to the body of the star. As the main feature of this design is the visual impact of the shape and colour, a visible texture is less important. It is more about the play of light over the coloured surface. Therefore you need a relatively smooth surface. This will also highlight the texture of the reflective edging.

Creating the foil edging is also more about a faceted surface that has an interesting effect with light rather than recreating a texture in scale form. The raw surface of the mount board is inherently suitable to take aerosol spray paint. However, in case there are any small deposits of glue or grease, it is advisable to spray the surface with a very light coat of white primer. You can use a specialist product from an art suppliers or the cheaper variety from a car accessories shop. If you miss this stage out, you may end up with a patchy surface. Once that is completely dry it is time to apply the colour.

PROJECT: MORE COMPLEX FORMS

When this is thoroughly dry, it is time to add the edging. As you are covering the edges of the model with foil, you don't need to mask the sides. In fact there is an advantage to the colour going slightly over the edges. You should apply the foil edging as neatly and accurately as possible, following the edge of the model. However, if there is a slight gap between the facia and the edging, then the overlapping of the paint will help the eye 'read' a perfect meeting point.

Before you apply the foil edging, remove the first part of the protective backing from the double-sided tape. Don't remove all of it or it will become unmanageable. Use the tip of your scalpel to tease the backing off, then your fingers to peel away a little more. Now apply the exposed, sticky part of the tape to one of the points where the star begins. Slowly guide the foil strip along the edge, gently pulling it taut so that it reaches the top of the point. Then gently fold it over the point and down other side. Make sure you pull it taut so that you retain the sharp point. Peel away a bit more of the protective layer and continue until you reach the end of that point. You can use your small metal rule to ease the foil strip into the inner angle. All the while you are applying the foil strip, apply light pressure only on the immediate area that you are sticking, while gently pulling the rest of the strip away from the edge.

This process can be tricky! The first time you try it, practise on a spare piece of card before working on the model. Only by doing this will you find the right way to co-ordinate your fingers and the sticky surface of the tape. Don't worry about getting it right first time. Just try it.

Once you have applied the strip to the whole edge of the star, go over it one more time with your fingers, smoothing it on. Make sure the edges of the strip are firmly in place. If for any reason you have overlapped the foil strip onto the main facia of the star, use a very sharp blade and your metal rule to trim off the excess.

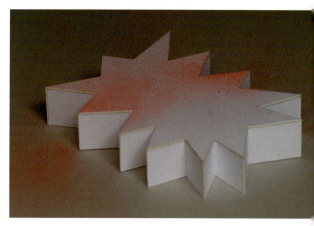

Build up colour with spray paint using several fine layers.

Hold the can a good distance away to avoid applying too much paint at once.

Using the main design to create new shapes.

Using coloured card and spray painted Bristol board.

Half the art of good model making is knowing how to deal with these discrepancies. Don't think about these things as mistakes. They are part of the process of using different materials. All materials behave in certain ways that are sometimes unpredictable. Don't let this put you off or think that you are doing something wrong. It is all about practice and technique. Try and get a sense of working with the material.

Designing and cutting out the layers

Now the main part of the model is complete you can add the finishing touches. The example shown uses some gold, metallic surfaced Bristol board and a home-made silver surfaced card. This was done by spraying some Bristol board with an aluminium effect spray paint. The shapes are based on the main star design. You can do this by tracing out the main design onto the Bristol

PROJECT: MORE COMPLEX FORMS   **43**

board. Then draw the new shape to fit inside it. As before, cut out the shape using a series of cuts, always beginning where the lines meet to form the points then and cut away from the point.

Attaching the layers

This type of layered detail lends itself to the use of spray or display mount. As with spray paint, do this in a well-ventilated area and hold the can a good distance away. Put the item to be glued on some newspaper. Apply the spray mount in one or two light layers. Carefully pick up the shape at the edges and gently put it in place. You may want to use your scalpel to lift the shape off the newspaper.

If you don't have spray mount, you could use double-sided tape. Apply it to the whole of the back surface of the Bristol board before cutting out the shape, just as you did with the foil strip. For the quickest, cleanest method just add a piece of double-sided tape to the centre of the shape then peel it back and stick it on. This is a little less permanent than the first two methods as the paper or card may curl up at the edges. However it is perfectly adequate for a presentational model or maquette.

Applying the shapes with double-sided tape.

The completed exploding star.

CHAPTER FIVE 45

PROJECT:
Making a Model Chair

FINE DETAILED WORK

A Chippendale chair

A Chippendale chair has been chosen as an example of how to make a piece of scale model furniture at 1:25 because of the delicacy of the design and also because of the necessity to get the scale absolutely right so that it reads properly and is a believable object. This project is a great way to practise and demonstrate your ability to make something of great delicacy.

However, to attempt to make this at 1:50 scale would be very difficult indeed. If achieved it would be a remarkable example of fine model-making technique, but would all the hard work really be visible? This book is concerned with techniques that help you to clearly communicate design ideas and create models and small sculptural forms that can clearly be seen and are a delight to look at. Fine technique is the route to that and not just an end in itself.

You may be daunted by this task as it does require very fine cutting and patient work. However, the techniques needed to make the cube and the star shape are part of the task, so, if you have practised these basic techniques already, you are on the path to creating more intricate work.

OPPOSITE: **Creating a fine piece of furniture.**

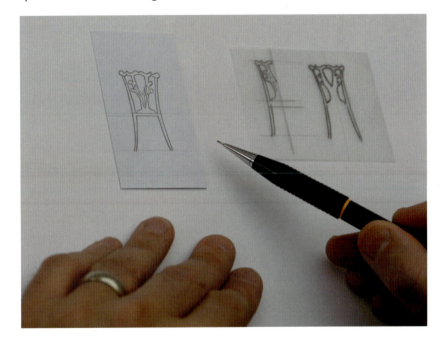

RIGHT: **Designing to scale.**

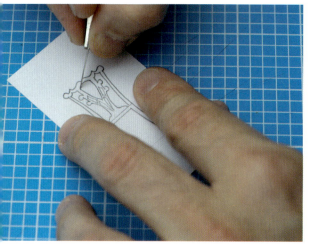

Carefully cutting out to create very fine work.

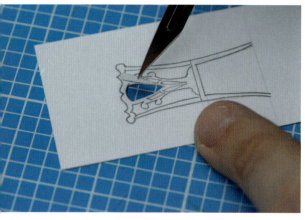

Removing the card with the tip of the blade.

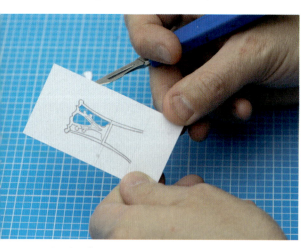

Reviewing your progress.

Begin by establishing the design and overall size of the model. Having found out the actual dimensions of the chair, mark them out to scale, using your scale ruler, on a piece of paper. Divide your drawing into areas. First mark out the total height from the floor to the top of the back of the chair. Draw a dividing line indicating where the seat of the chair goes. Draw a line down the centre of this mark out. Using your click pencil, lightly draw in the curved design and the curved legs on one half of the centre line. Bear in mind that though you are creating fine work, you will be cutting out voids in the card to create the curls and curves of the wood. So make sure that the voids aren't so close together that when you come to cut them out, the card that remains will break or tear. These remaining areas can be as thin as half a millimetre if you use a very sharp blade; almost like thread. However this also depends on the thickness of the card you will use. Do not attempt fine work like this using mount board. It has to be Bristol board.

Once you have completed drawing one half of the design, trace over it. Include the centre line. Then reverse the tracing paper and draw over it on the other side of the centre line to transfer a mirror image. Now you have an accurate and symmetrical design.

Now trace the complete design onto a piece of Bristol board that is cut to a workable size. This may be quite small so you can always lightly attach it to your cutting mat with some small pieces of masking tape.

Cutting out

As with the cube and the star, gently insert the point of a sharp scalpel blade into the corner where two lines meet, and very lightly score along the line of your drawing. Having done that, add a little more pressure on the second cut. A third scoring will most likely be sufficient to enable you to remove the void. Imagine you are drawing with the point of the blade rather than cutting. Feel the card giving way and delight in the detailed work that is appearing before your eyes.

Take your time and never attempt to cut out the shapes in one go except when cutting out the tiniest shapes. The best method is to use the tip of the blade like a pin to prick the shape out.

When removing the shapes, use the tip of the blade – they will be too small for your fingers! Work your way out from the centre of the design, cutting out the outer shape of the whole chair last. Move the card around so that the angle of the blade and direction of cutting is predominantly going from top to bottom, left to right. Try not to twist your wrist into awkward positions. After a few cuts, flex your fingers a few times to keep your hands feeling relaxed.

Once you have cut out the back of the chair, draw out and trace the front legs and cut them out using the same technique, 'drawing' gently with the scalpel.

Measure and draw out the seat using these methods too. However, this can be made of two layers of mount board. Cut the two layers separately and join them together using a little PVA or double-sided tape. Then lightly sand the seat all around the edge. To represent the cushioned area that sits within a seat, add a layer or two of Bristol board, cut slightly smaller than the seat. Use double-sided tape to attach it.

If you were making a deeply upholstered seat or sofa, you could use some 3mm or 5mm foam board. Remove the top, paper surface, then gently sand the top surface of the foam and round off the edges. When you come to paint it, use a little gesso or white emulsion as a primer. You could lightly stipple the surface too as this gives a fabric-like effect.

Having cut out all three main parts of the chair, first stick the seat to the back of the chair and then the front legs to the seat. Use PVA glue or a little dab of UHU®. Don't use UHU® directly from the tube as you may accidentally squeeze too hard

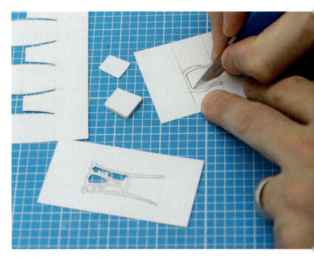
Cutting out the legs.

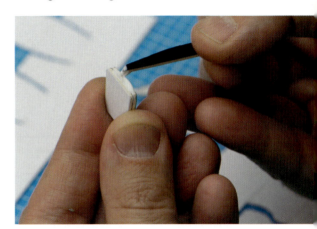
Applying PVA to the seat.

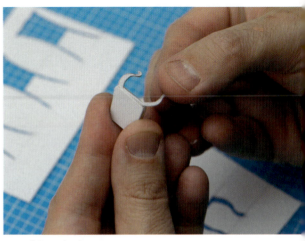
Attaching the legs.

and ruin your intricate work. Dispense a little UHU® onto some card or a plastic palette and use a toothpick or sliver of card as an applicator.

Once you have attached these pieces, gently tease the back of the chair into a curve. Do this by holding the sides of the seat between finger and thumb and then smoothing the back of the chair in an upward direction using the finger and thumb of your other hand.

Strengthening delicate work

Now put layers of newspaper or some type of absorbent paper such as sugar paper, under the model and coat it with the runny variety of Super Glue®. There is no totally clean way to do this. The main thing is to completely coat the model with glue without getting any on your fingers. All Super Glue® bonds flesh very quickly but the runny variety is almost instantaneous!

Do a little at a time by holding the model chair with the tips of your fingers or tweezers to hold it. Dispense a small droplet of glue onto the model. Let gravity help you and make sure that you hold the chair downwards and apply the glue so that it runs down the part of the model that is furthest from your fingers. Allow plenty of time for the runny glue to be absorbed into the card. Then apply another small droplet. This second drop of glue will sit slightly on the surface of the card until it is dry. Excess glue will drip off the model onto the paper below. This is unavoidable. Just be careful not to rest your hand in it by accident!

You can speed up the process by using glue accelerator. Either use the spray variety or buy a syringe and apply it directly by dispensing a droplet from the syringe, having drawn some into it earlier. A more basic way to apply the accelerator is to dip a short piece of metal rod into the accelerator bottle and apply a droplet so that it makes contact with the gluey area.

Do take your time at this stage. If the glue is not dry, the model will stick to your fingers. This is not only tricky to remove from your skin, but you may damage the delicate Bristol board and you will have to start again!

The components of the chair bonded together before strengthening with Super Glue®.

Colouring

The best way to create a wood effect on the chair is to use wood stain. Depending how the glue has been absorbed into the card and how it has dried on the surface, you may need to cut away some virtually microscopic fronds or bumps of excess glue. You need to do this or they will show up when you apply the wood stain. Use a very sharp scalpel or even a mini file to gently file it away. Once the glue is dry the model will be more robust, though take care, as the legs can be brittle and can easily snap.

Before adding the wood stain you may want to prime the model. Use some watered-down gesso and a small, soft brush to apply a 'wash' primer. Once that is dry, apply another watery layer if you want a solid finish. Take great care not to fill any little cut out parts of the design or to allow the gesso to form tiny lumps on the edges. Gently blow on it to dry the gesso and remove any excess in the voids. You can also use a clean, dry, soft brush to remove any unwanted primer.

When this is dry apply the wood stain in stages rather like you did with the Super Glue®. Avoid staining your fingers and keep working over the protective paper underneath, to protect your cutting mat or work surface. You may think it would be useful to wear protective gloves, but the work is so tiny that gloves restrict your ability to create fine work.

Other detailing

It may be desirable to add a little thickness to the legs of the chair. This can be done before the priming stage, or after, by adding a tiny sliver of modelling material such as fine grade Miliput® or Plasticine to the tops of the legs. Use a sanded toothpick or piece of metal rod and your fingers, to apply it and smooth it round the front of the legs at their widest part. You will only need a very small amount of

Applying wood stain.

modelling material. A little more runny Super Glue® or even some PVA painted over it, will be sufficient to fix it. Add the gesso primer on top, as described above.

You can then re-apply a little primer to the upholstered seat area then paint it with gouache or use an acrylic paint directly onto it. The consistency is thicker than gouache so you don't always need primer.

Tips for mass production

It is worth knowing that if you need to make a lot of these chairs or similar (I once had to make a whole dining set of twenty Chippendales and fifty plastic garden chairs!) it is best to set up a production line: draw all the components out first. You could print off the design several times and spray mount them onto the Bristol board, though this won't work for extremely fine work because it will make the thickness of the Bristol board unworkable.

While there is no point becoming obsessed with process, the idea is to learn and practise these techniques to produce wonderful models, as well as enjoying this process of model making as well as the results.

CHAPTER SIX

PROJECT:
Making an Organic Form

A TREE

When I began model making, I thought about the things I didn't have any idea how to make. A tree was one of them. Nobody told me how to do this so the method that follows, is my method. You may come up with your own. Begin by using some of the techniques you have looked at already but for different effects this time.

Start by drawing out your tree design. Imagine it in profile and develop a bold and pleasing shape. Trace it out, then transfer that to a suitable piece of mount board that will contain the whole design.

As with the chair, cut away the 'voids' to reveal the branches. Begin where the lines meet in a point and cut away from the point. Don't attempt to cut the twists and turns of the branches in one stroke or even try to score out the whole shape first. This time, divide the task of cutting the irregular shape of the branches into a series of angular cuts. Gradually add detail by cutting into the corners and angles. Do this once you have completed creating the main shape of one branch at a time. Move the card around to suit your hand movements. This is all about dividing up the task into simple cuts.

When you have cut out all the branches, move on to cut out the trunk. Already you can see the tree developing. Draw and cut out the profile of the tree trunk and glue this to the front of the trunk with PVA or UHU®. You can attach this profile before you cut out the trunk and the outer branches if you like, as it will give you something to hold onto as you work your way around the tree.

Once these stages are complete, draw and cut out a base to the trunk and glue in place. You can be liberal with the glue as these profiles will be covered up.

Now you start to flesh out the model by adding bits of Plasticine to the trunk, smoothing it between the trunk profile and main cut out. You can add a little at time by rolling out Plasticine sausages and squeezing them into place. If you have added too much, cut it away, retaining the profile of the trunk as a guide.

Continue adding thickness by smoothing a little Plasticine up into the first part of the branches. This will give a real feeling of the branches growing out of the trunk. As you

OPPOSITE: **A tree set against a back drop.**

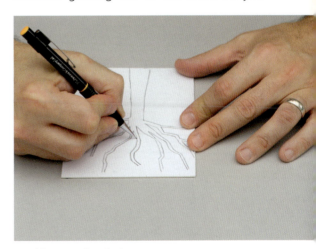

Marking out the design.

PROJECT: MAKING AN ORGANIC FORM

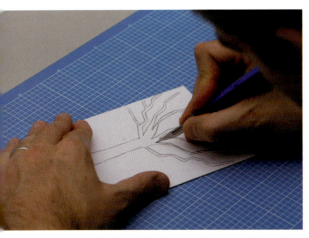

Cut out the branches by cutting away from the trunk.

model, think of the organic quality of a tree and imagine it growing. In all model making it is important to devote yourself completely to the task in hand. Focus all your thoughts into the process and have the end vision in your mind. By practising like this you will automatically find that you come up with new techniques that are revealed to you as you work.

Now let's strengthen the model and help create a surface that you can work into to create texture. Paint the Plasticine with some PVA and extend this to the branches. This is a process of unifying the different materials you are using to create the whole object.

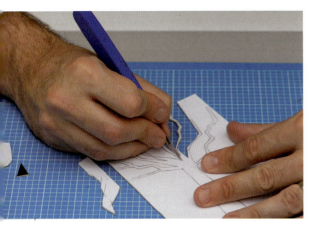

Work your way from the centre.

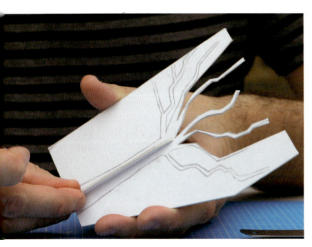

Adding a profile.

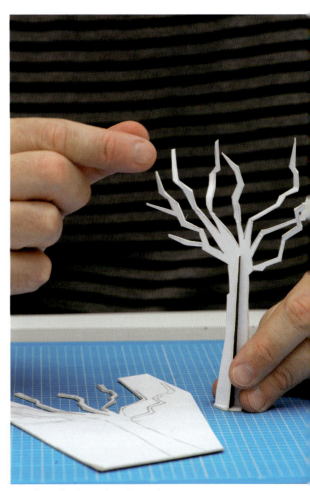

Bending the branches into shape.

PROJECT: MAKING AN ORGANIC FORM 53

Adding Plasticine to flesh out the trunk.

Using rough parcel string as a material.

When the PVA is dry, you could work some texture into the Plasticine by scraping into it with a toothpick or running an old scalpel blade down it at an angle. Use a wire brush or anything that will create texture. Because you are using a pliable product, you can always smooth back some of the textural marks you have made to soften the effect. Once you think you have gone as far as you can with this process, apply another thin layer of PVA to seal everything.

Adding other materials

Now start to add some other materials: string, wire and tissue paper. The rough variety of thin parcel string is wonderfully fibrous and ideal for building up layers of bark. Cut some lengths slightly shorter than the trunk and separate the woven fibres by untwisting the string with your fingers. Then use your scalpel to tease apart the finer fibres. The string will start to resemble hair. Don't deconstruct the piece of string entirely. Apply a teased length of string to the trunk, building up from the base. Let the loose fronds overlap the base of the trunk, forming roots. Use your fingers to put the string in place and then add enough pressure with a small, stiff brush to keep it in place while the PVA starts to go off.

Once you think you have enough of this material, start to add the tissue paper. Do this by cutting some small strips then rolling them up so that they resemble a thin, hand-rolled cigarette. Twist it tightly. In a way this is the opposite process to what you have done with the string. Now add the fronds of tissue paper over and around the string on the trunk. Let some pieces overlap the base as well, forming more roots.

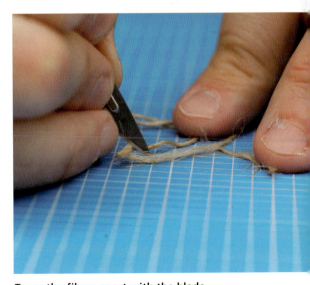

Tease the fibres apart with the blade.

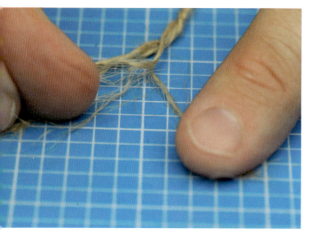

Separate the fibres.

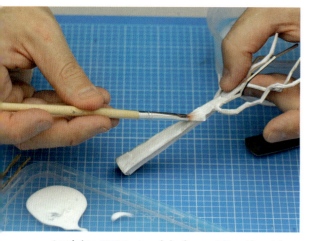

Applying PVA to trunk before adding the string.

Applying the string with more PVA.

Finally add some thin wire. You can use copper wire or varying thicknesses of fuse wire. Do this once the string and tissue paper is fully stuck and the PVA has dried. Use UHU® to attach the wire. You can be quite free with this process. On this occasion, the stringy quality of the glue is an advantage and will add yet more texture.

Make sure that you have extended all these materials onto the branches. To help with scale, add more string at the base and wire at the top of the trunk and on the branches. Use the tissue paper to bridge the two materials. You could also add some small flat pieces of tissue paper, torn into strips. Lay them over the top of all these materials randomly, leaving some of the twists of string, twisted paper and wire exposed and covering some areas up.

Use stringy fronds of UHU® at the base of the branches to integrate the wire and card. Finally add some short pieces of the thinnest wire to the ends of the branches. If you want to add leaves, this is where you would attach them. You could use UHU® or Super Glue®. You can make your own leaves from paper or buy a metal etched one that can be twisted into shape, or try a combination of both.

This project is to make a rather sinister and barren tree, where the formation of the branches and the texture of the bark is the predominant part of the design. Once the wire has been attached to the branches, you can start to bend them so that they look like they are growing out at different angles. The thin wire and rubbery nature of the UHU® will allow you to do this. This is the part where the tree really starts to come together.

When you are happy that you have added enough texture, and all the adhesives have fully cured, it is time to add a primer coat.

This is primarily about creating a surface that will take the paint. It is not necessary to coat it with a completely opaque layer of primer. It is good to allow some of the natural colour of the string to bleed through. Even tiny, exposed sections of the wire could read as highlights and make the model more realistic.

PROJECT: MAKING AN ORGANIC FORM

Using twists of tissue paper.

Mixing tissue paper and string to form bark texture and roots.

When the primer is dry, add a wash of your base colour. It is best to make this the darkest tone and get it into the areas between the different textures.

If you use acrylic paint for the base colour, once it is dry it is fixed. Next build up more layers with washes of acrylic or gouaches mixed with a little PVA. Once you have finished this stage and the paints are fully dry, you can add small amounts of thicker paint using the dry brush technique. A small, stiff brush is good for detailed highlights and lowlights as well as flecks of contrasting colour.

Use a large, soft brush with a very small amount of paint that is virtually dry and brush over the whole model. This will really unify your work and it will bring out all the textures at the same time.

There is no need to restrict yourself to using paint. Coloured pencils with water-soluble leads are excellent for adding really fine, colour detail. Use the pencil lead on its side and roll it over the raised areas on the model. Vary the pressure as you go and add as many tones as you like.

Building up the detail.

Applying a base colour.

Adding highlights using water-soluble pencils.

Adding a setting

Having made your tree a freestanding, descriptive object with roots growing out at the base of the trunk, you could develop the idea further and construct a setting for it.

A way to do this is to cut a circle out of a piece of foam board. Use the same technique as cutting it out of mount board. Draw the circle with a pair of compasses then 'draw' freehand, using your scalpel to break through the paper surface. Now make a deeper incision with the blade carefully tracing the circle. A third or fourth revolution with the blade may be necessary. All the while keep the blade at the same angle and feel it break through the foam and into the bottom layer of paper. If you want a pristine and perfect circular base, lightly sand the circumference. You could choose to work into it and create a section of landscape. Cut away at the front edges and sculpt the foam surface by taking slices out of it. Once you have completed this, cut away enough of the foam in the centre to locate the tree. Glue it in with PVA or if you have used Kapa board you can glue it in place with UHU®.

You can make little holes in the surface of the foam board with a small piece of metal rod to embed the roots. It is also possible to make little cuts in the surface and squeeze the roots into them. Add more PVA over the top along with tiny shreds of tissue paper. Stick this in place and wrinkle it up. Add some sand or crumbly cork texture if you like.

When the tree is firmly stuck in place, prime the base and add a base green. Add washes and dry-brushed paint as you did with the tree. You can buy a green, powdery texture to sprinkle over an area that has been painted with PVA. Use it sparingly to give a mossy feel to the base.

PROJECT: MAKING AN ORGANIC FORM   57

Showing the tree in stages.

You could also stick some to the roots and the bottom half of the trunk too to really integrate the base with the trunk.

Now think about a background. As we have a curved base, we need to construct a cyclorama. Bristol board would easily bend to fit around the curve of the base though one layer would not be very strong. It is possible to laminate two or three layers together but it is best to have something more robust.

To do this, first decide how high you want your cyclorama and how far it wraps around the base. Cut a piece of mount board that is high enough but a bit wider than you need. You can guess the width or curve a length of string around the base and take your measurement from that.

You now need to score the back of the card with vertical lines so that it will curve easily around the base. The width between the vertical scores will depend on the circumference of your base.

Fully textured and coloured, attached to a circular base.

PROJECT: MAKING AN ORGANIC FORM

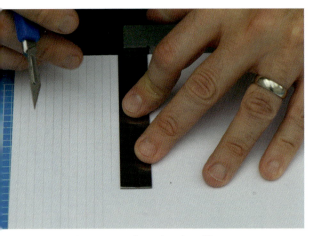

Scoring mount board so it will curve.

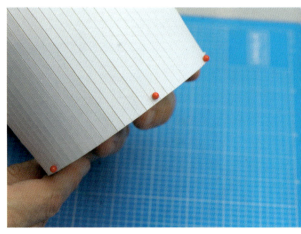

Pins will keep everything in place until the glue dries.

Fitting scored mount board around the base.

The model is almost complete.

PROJECT: MAKING AN ORGANIC FORM

Finished tree complete with coloured cyclorama.

However, the more scores there are, the more flexible the mount board will be. Use a ruler to make the equidistant marks then use your try square to mark out the base of the vertical lines. Once you have done this all along the card, complete the scores using a metal rule. Apply just enough pressure with the blade to cut about a third of the way through the card. Once you have done this, try flexing the card into a curve. If it is still too resistant, then go over the scored lines as necessary.

The design on the cyclorama should not detract from the high level of detail on the tree. You could use spray paint to build up layers of tone and colour and create a hazy sky or eerie mist. It is best to do this before you start scoring.

The cyclorama needn't have a straight top. Cut into it to add drama to your landscape. Maybe cut a separate strip to make a lower horizon. This will sit at the base of the cyclorama and will visually link the circular base and the two design elements.

Attach the cyclorama by first applying a line of PVA along the bottom and then pin it in place. Use long pins with plastic heads. While this is drying, cut out the detail of the lower horizon. Stick this to the main cyclorama using UHU® as a contact adhesive. That way the two curves will firmly adhere to each other. The tree is now complete.

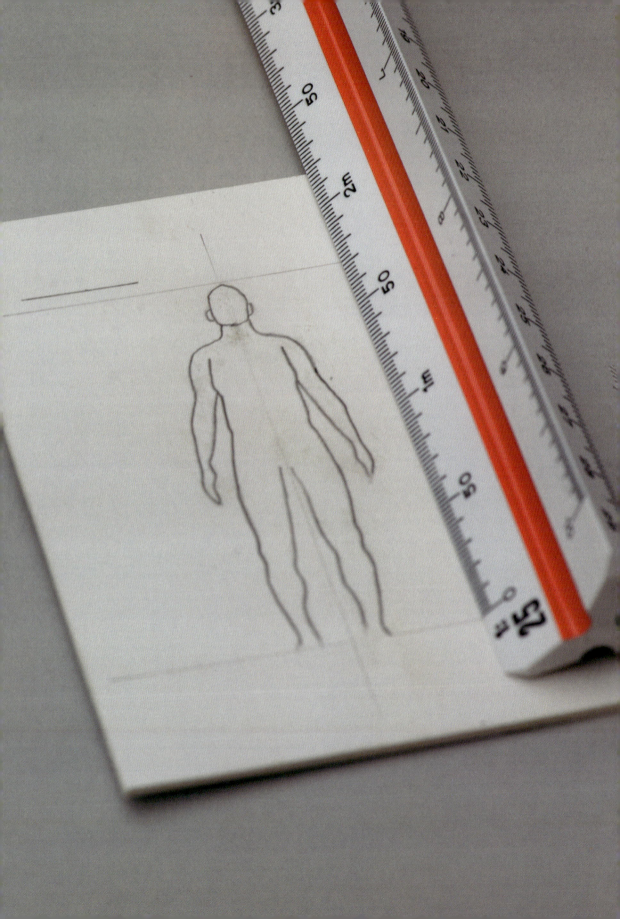

CHAPTER SEVEN 61

PROJECT:
A Human Figure in 1:25 Scale

GETTING THE SCALE RIGHT

More than any other project, this is one where a good sense of scale is essential. Making a human figure is rather like a life drawing class. You have to get the proportions of the human absolutely right or it just won't read.

How to begin

Start by constructing a simple skeleton with the correct proportions of the human body. This will be constructed out of copper wire. It is very flexible and thin enough to be bent and shaped as is necessary.

If you are good at drawing, mark out a human figure on a piece of card. Alternatively find an image of a person standing upright and reproduce it to scale 1:25. You could choose da Vinci's Vitruvian Man.

Take a length of copper wire but don't cut it. It is quite difficult to know exactly how much you will need and once it is cut there is no going back.

Begin by forming the arm and a shoulder. Bend the wire to form the arm, then loop it back up the arm and across the neck to form the other shoulder. Continue down to form the other arm then back up again. At this point, or even slightly before, twist the wire together so that the parallel

OPPOSITE: **Using a drawing of a 1:25 figure as a guide.**

Drawing out the figure to get a sense of scale.

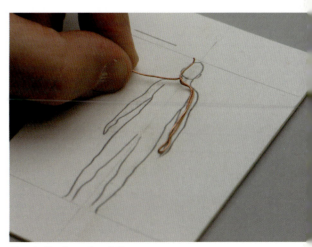

Check the length of the arm as you go.

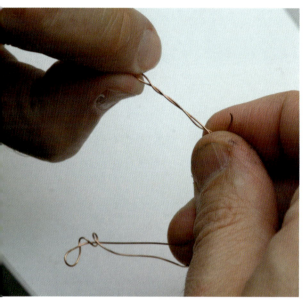

Twisting the copper wire.

strands become one, intertwined limb. Check the length of the arms against your figure drawing as you go.

When you reach back up to the neck, form a spine then bend to form a hip bone. Bend again to make a leg, checking the length against your drawing. Form a heel by making a tiny loop before forming a foot. This is formed of a longer loop. Now continue back up the leg, across the hip and down, to make the other leg and foot. You can make a large loop at the heel. This can act as a stand for your completed figure. Finish the skeleton by continuing up the leg to the hip and cut at the base of the spine. Twist the end around the base: the skeleton is complete.

If you have got the scale right, this simple, stick man will already be very expressive; like a miniature Giacometti sculpture, but with more

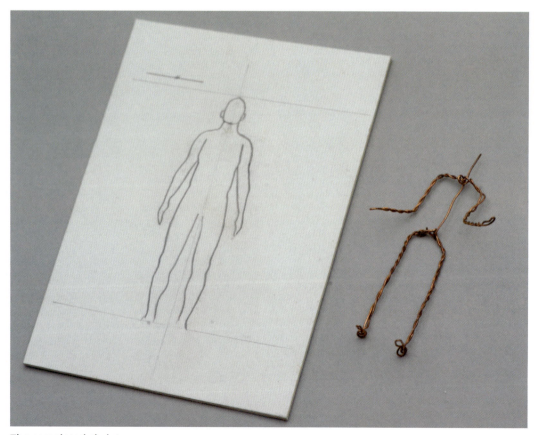

The completed skeleton.

PROJECT: A HUMAN FIGURE IN 1:25 SCALE

realistic proportions. Of course, you can play with proportion once you know how to achieve a more realistically formed human figure.

Fleshing it out

The next stage is to add some body to the skeleton. Begin by coating the wire skeleton with a thin layer of modelling material. When you first make a figure use Plasticine rather than another material. It is the simplest material to use. Make tiny 'sausages' of Plasticine and twist them onto the wire. Then smooth them in place. You don't have to know all the complex anatomy of the human body but a little knowledge does help because now you are going to build up a version of the musculature.

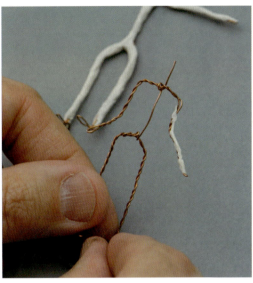

Starting to flesh out the body.

Begin by forming two little balls of Plasticine and partially flatten them in place to make the chest. Wrap some pieces below the chest, around the spine, to make ribs and a stomach. Build up shoulder blades at the back and form the buttocks. Now add some tiny fronds to the front and back of the legs. Then do the same for the arms. Allow plenty of time to make your figure. As well as concentrating on forming the details of the body, you need to fix the Plasticine as you go with a little PVA. Paint it on using a small, soft brush. It will form a skin-like layer

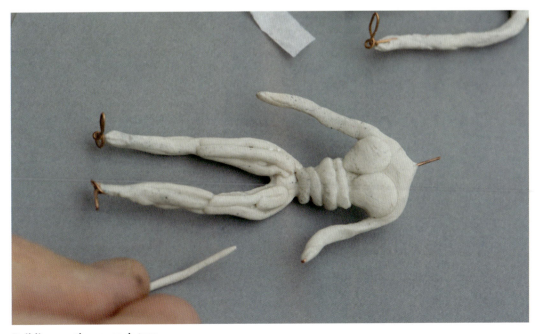

Building up the musculature.

and help keep the musculature from become too homogenized. Add a little Plasticine to form the feet but don't worry about the details of the hands at this stage.

Dressing the figure

It may seem crazy to have spent all this time building up details of the body when you are about to cover it up. However, the principle is the same when drawing or painting a clothed figure. You need to sketch out the body's inner structure to get the figure right.

The details of this next stage depend on how the figure is to be dressed, but the basic method is the same. Use tissue paper, cut and torn into tiny strips, to make trousers. Bind the legs by first applying a little PVA to the figure. Let the tissue paper soak up the glue as you wrap it around the legs. Form sleeves in the same way. Add creases at the shoulders and knees by rolling very thin pieces of Plasticine and bend these over the tissue paper and fix with PVA. Build up the front panels of a tailored jacket by cutting out the shape in tissue paper and sticking it on. Add more Plasticine if necessary to build up the shoulders or base of the jacket. Make collars, pocket flaps, cuffs and reveres out of newspaper or cheap, white paper. Crisp little details like these really draw the eye and make the figure realistic.

Form the head by starting to build up the neck then sitting a little ball of Plasticine that is smaller in scale than a whole head, onto the wire neck. Smooth them together. Next add another little, smaller, ball to the back of the head to form a skull-like shape and add a tiny piece for the chin. Smooth into shape using the very tips of your fingers; a blunt, rounded, hard, pencil or modelling tool.

Make little indentations to form the cheeks. You can add the nose by cutting the tiniest of profiles out of Bristol board and sticking it on with glue. Smooth a little of the 'face' to join this nose. Integrate all this by painting some PVA over the whole head, letting the glue gather around the features.

Integrate the clothes by joining areas of Plasticine and paper by laying little torn layers of tissue paper over the top. The torn edges create, soft, seamless joins. Once this is done, paint the whole figure with a final coat of PVA. You can use a hair dryer to accelerate the glue drying process between coats.

Adding tissue paper with PVA.

Priming and painting

Add a thin layer of gesso or watered down emulsion as a primer, being careful not to lose any detail. When this is dry, paint your figure using a brush with long, soft bristles. Put on a base wash and allow to dry. Then add another wash of colour that is a tone lighter. You can work in surprisingly broad strokes to achieve a great effect. You

Forming the details of the clothes.

can add fine detail later, using a very fine brush to pick out buttons or features. However if you add too much detail, the eye will only see painted effects. The figure will appear static, like an old-fashioned toy soldier. These toy soldiers and railway sets are an art form in themselves. But with this method of constructing and painting a figure, you are learning a different skill – to bring the figure to life.

Think about how you position the limbs when building up the figure. The position of the hands is incredibly important. It tells us something of the intention of the figure. We should have an idea of where the figure was and where it is about to go. Think about this as you make it. How will the arm pull back at a particular moment? How will this affect the sleeve of the jacket in which it is covered?

Adding primer with a soft brush.

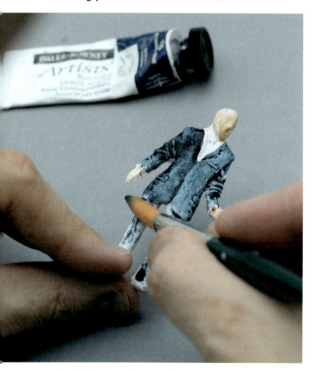

Applying a colour wash.

Make the hands in the same way as the nose. Cut out the main shape of the hand, separating the thumb and possibly some of the fingers. Stick these tiny profiles on the ends of the arms and use enough PVA to build up the paper and round off the edges.

Beware of painting the face and hands, or any exposed areas of flesh with too heavy a coat of paint. Paint these areas like the clothes. Build up in washes, using a light, free stroke. Don't think about painting every little finger or nostril. Think about what the figure is doing and you will find yourself adding a wash of colour here, a hint of a detail there, without really thinking about it and the figure will come alive!

PROJECT: A HUMAN FIGURE IN 1:25 SCALE   67

The painting is complete.

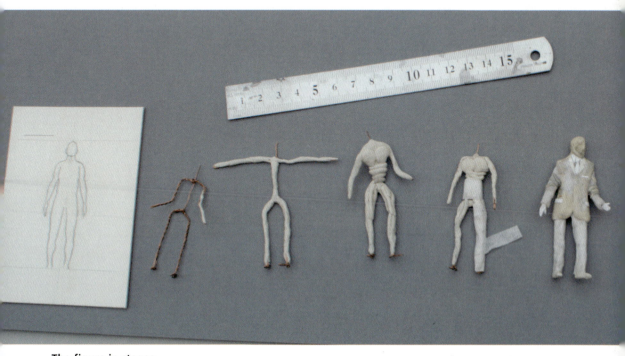

The figure in stages.

CHAPTER EIGHT

PROJECT:
An Architectural Environment

AN ELEGANT PANELLED ROOM WITH FLOORBOARDS

NOT an architect's model!

The subheading above is not intended to be critical of architects' models. The people who make them are highly skilled; you may want to make them yourself! Many of the techniques and information in this book about tools and materials, would help you to do so. But, as with the model figure, the approach here is to create a model with life and atmosphere, as well as conveying more tangible, factual information about proportion, scale and texture.

You need to begin with the basic structure. The best material to use for the walls is foam board. In this project you will use a variety that has a grey paper surface. You will recreate panelling using Bristol board. You will see that, on the interior section of the model, you won't be painting these materials because I want to demonstrate that accurate work with raw materials can still breathe life into a model, even without colour washes and sophisticated paint techniques.

Begin by cutting the foam board in a strip that is the height of the walls. Then divide the strip into the separate walls. Use your try square for perfect right angles. Next, mark out the portals that form the doorways and windows. Use a click pencil to lightly indicate their size and positions. Then gently score the surface of the foam board. Whenever working on any project that involves any marking out and cutting into the material, remember: measure twice, cut once!

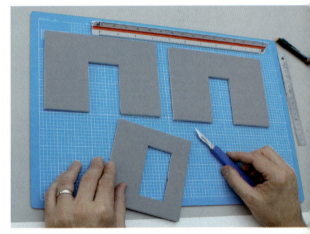

Walls with portals made from foam board.

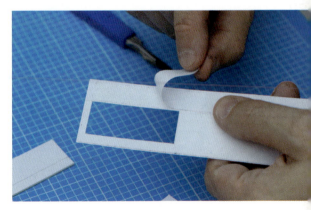

Using double-sided tape to build up layers of panelling.

OPPOSITE: **A figure in its context; an architectural space.**

Begin by cutting out the portals from the corners. After scoring, two or three incisions will cut through the foam board. Make sure you get into the corners. Think about which wall will join up where, and trim the length accordingly as you did when making the cube, to take into account the thickness of the foam board and how it will affect the length of the wall. When you have completed this part of the process, put these pieces to one side.

Doors, windows and frames

Use mount board to make the doors, their frames and the windows. Again mark out the main dimensions and cut them out. Mark out the inner dimensions and cut them out by working from the centre out.

When cutting out the door frame, keep the piece of card that will become the door in a safe place while you build up the layers of the frame. Make the panelling in the same way, marking and cutting out the main sections from mount board and then doing the same on the Bristol board for the layers. Use two or three layers of Bristol board on top of the mount board. Make sure that the panelling sits slightly back of the door and window frames.

Before cutting out the voids, back the Bristol board with double-sided tape. Build up the layers of Bristol board before attaching the completed panelling to the walls. Attach the door frames to the walls before attaching the panelling. This will help you locate the frame around the portal accurately. It will also help position the panelling in relation to the frame. You can use a combination of tape and UHU® on the back of the panelling. You may want to add the skirting last of all. Before actually sticking any of the architectural details down, lay the pieces in position to check that they are all in the correct place.

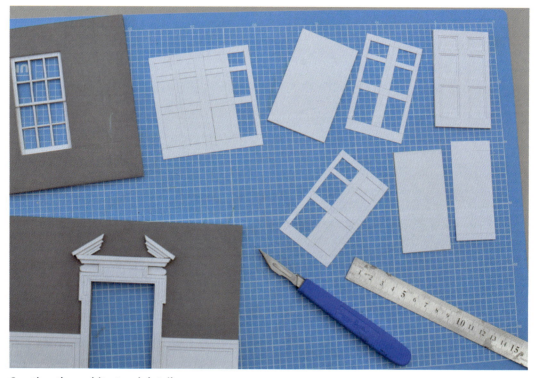

Creating the architectural detail.

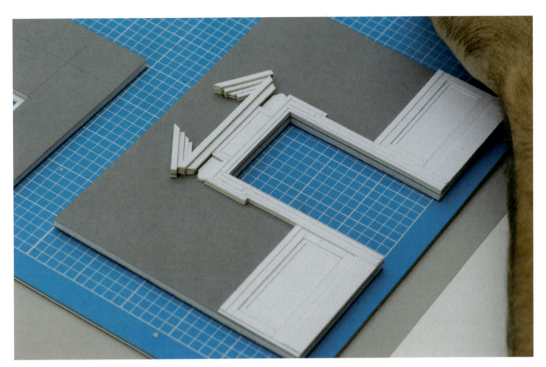

Frame and panelling complete.

If you plan to paint the panelling with washes, it is best to add a little glue to all the layers. Always prime the card first before applying gouache. When you cut into any card, the edge will be raw. This means that the paint, particularly washes, will soak into the edges. Not only will the edges take on a darker appearance but it may weaken the bond between the layers. If you are using aerosol paint, there is less danger of this because of the consistency of the paint. However, a thin layer of primer will pull everything together.

If in doubt about any paint finish or texture, experiment on a spare piece of card. Make some extra panelling to try out effects. You could even keep these experimental pieces and make some notes, recording the process.

Throughout the project, keep your working area and hands clean. It is so easy to spoil your work with stains and smudges. If this does happen it is sometimes possible to remove them. First try using a good quality eraser. Make sure that it is clean so that you don't rub in more unwanted marks! If that doesn't work, try lightly scraping the surface of the card with a new blade. If you succeed in removing the offending smudge but there are visible scraping marks, go over it again with the eraser. There is only so much of this you can do, so it is best avoided if you can.

For really fine and detailed work, there are other ways to build up layers. You can make your own dado and picture rail using layers of Bristol board, but as the detail gets smaller it is possible to add strips of very thin piano wire to the card. Fix this on using medium consistency Super Glue®. You can wipe away any excess with a strip of Bristol board.

You can also buy ready-formed strips of it in wood as well as building up layers using white styrene strips. These are bonded together using a special solution known as plastic weld that

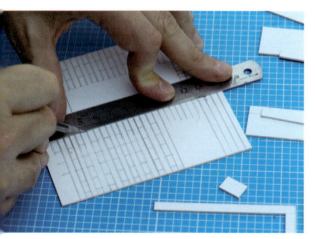
Scoring out the brick.

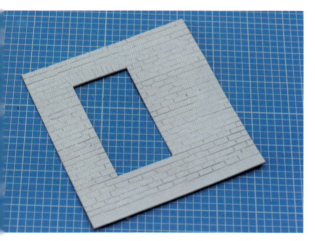
Brick wall scored and primed.

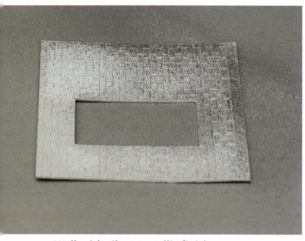
Wall with silver metallic finish.

you paint on. A chemical reaction occurs and the styrene molecules reform so that all the strips bond together.

If you use several types of material, it's best to do this with a project where you will paint the whole model. Priming will be essential so that all the materials have a consistent surface that takes the paint. A balance must be struck between use of materials, layers of priming and paint, and the retention of detail. The more layers of paint you add, the bigger the danger of dulling the sharpness of your work. Only experience and your own design aesthetic will tell you how far to go with each process.

On this project you are going to be judicious with your use of paint. The idea is to create contrast and distinguish interior from exterior. Though you will be looking to produce a recognizable brick surface for the exterior, the paint treatment will be quite bold and not naturalistic.

Before starting on a project like this, it is useful to have a knowledge of basic architectural styles. Become familiar with the size of doors and levels at which dado and picture rails sit. If in doubt, measure them in real life or do your research into the architectural style of which your model will be a representation.

As you design and construct the model, think about the whole house, not just the room or area you are representing. On the surface, this advice sounds rather abstract and unnecessary but it will inform the whole work in a very practical way.

For example, the positioning of a door directly relates to what is beyond it and where it leads. If you want to make a model of a beautiful room but you don't consider where the room is in relation to what is around it, then the model won't 'stand up'. It won't be based in any truth and therefore it somehow won't be believable. To subvert or twist reality to emphasize a certain feeling, you need to know where to start from.

When making the window, in this case a Georgian sash, it is important to know the correct proportions and relationship between the sections of glass and glazing bars. You may want the window to be slightly larger than life to communicate a certain feeling. This directly affects the choice of materials you may want to use to express the idea, and how much detail you can add. The conceptual and aesthetic concerns affect the practical, technical ones. In this case you are using mount board. On a larger design you could incorporate a Bristol board layer with thin piano wire. But for now, to the project in hand.

Having drawn out the window frame using your try square, cut out the voids to reveal the frame in this sequence: cut all the verticals first. Then make the horizontal cuts. Work into the corners so that the voids pop out in one go. Work carefully making sure you don't cut through the glazing bars. However, if you do, you can glue them back in place with a little PVA.

Once you have cut out a void for the window from the piece of card that will become the exterior brick wall, you could use this piece for the window frame as it will be exactly the right size. Hopefully, if your measuring and cutting has been accurate, the brick facia void and window void in the foam board will match exactly. You may need to lightly sand around the inner edges of the foam board to ensure a good fit for the window frame. It should be a snug fit but the frame mustn't buckle.

Creating a wall of brick is an unavoidably slow process. You can buy pressed plastic sheets of brick pattern but these do have their limitations. They have a repetitive and manufactured feel to them and only stand up to a minimal amount of colouring because the imprint is quite shallow. Far better to make your own. All the effort will be worth it.

Begin by marking out the rows of brick. Start from the top of the card. This is because the height of your card may not correspond to an exact number of seams of brick. If this is the case, a row of half bricks sits better visually at the base of a model than the top. You

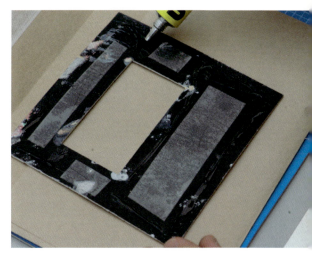

Applying double-sided tape and UHU© to brick wall.

can also incorporate a type of exterior skirting into your design too, if this is appropriate. Alternatively, determine the height of your wall before you start by getting the measurement of a brick and calculate how many seams it will take to construct the height that you like. Don't forget to include the lines of mortar between the seams.

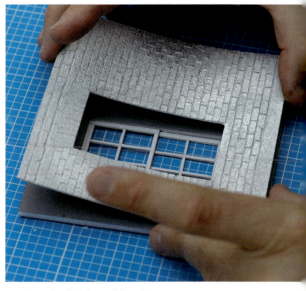

Putting the brick wall in place.

The completed exterior wall.

Mark out the rows by first measuring their position with the scale ruler. Then using your try square, work your way up the wall. Having done this, extend the lines using your metal rule and a very fine pencil. As you mark out the seams in full, keep checking that the rows are completely horizontal and that the spaces between them are exactly equal. It is awful to get to the top of the wall only to discover that the rows are gradually sloping upwards or downwards. This will be immediately obvious once you carve out the mortar lines and you will have to start again. It will also affect the next stage, which is to mark out the vertical lines of mortar.

When you have done and you are happy with it, it's time to carve out the mortar. Start with the horizontal seams. Using a very sharp blade and your metal rule, score along the drawn line. You don't have to start at the bottom or the top. This task is very repetitive and it is important to keep your concentration as you do it. You could start in the middle and then score two parallel lines to form a line of mortar, then count five seams down and break up the task in this way.

When scoring, turn the card around so that the left side of the model becomes the top. Work from top to bottom. Having scored two parallel lines, go back to the top and carefully pick out the thin sliver of card between the lines. The top surface should give way and the sliver will curl up and out. It will reveal a very thin, pulpy line and the top surface of the mount board will be thrown forward in relief.

Having completed all the lines, turn the card back in position so that you now have horizontal rows. Now begin to cut the verticals. This is even more painstaking work! This is because the lines are so short and you must avoid scoring too far. You don't want to cut into the row of bricks below.

While it is a necessarily slow process, you will be impressed and encouraged to continue as you see the bricks start to emerge. There will

A planked floor.

be a natural variation to the depth of your scored mortar lines. This is good because such a variation occurs in real brick walls. As you progress, imagine the wall growing as you go. Allow the process to become an enjoyable one rather than a chore. Delight in the contradiction between the very lightweight material that you are using and illusion of solidity and weight that you are creating. Good model making is a lot about the thought that goes into it. It is not merely the knowledge of materials and practice of techniques.

When you have scored out the basic brick pattern, you now have the opportunity to add even more character. Using the tip of your blade, round off the corners on some of the bricks. You can choose how many of these you want to do as you go. Do it randomly, possibly working in clusters of predominantly odd numbers. Slope the scalpel handle so that the blade trims off the edges of some of the bricks, rather like the method used for chamfering. Use your metal rule as a guide on some bricks and work freehand on others.

For larger areas of brick, more of this detailing is necessary. You can manufacture some extra rows of brick and cut them into individual ones. These can then be halved in depth by peeling off the bottom layer. Choose where you want them to go by placing them on your wall a few at a time. Then stick them on using PVA.

When laminating a foam board wall with brick, make sure your lines of mortar meet up at the corners! Hopefully this will happen because of your accurate measuring and scoring of the lines. However, you may find a few slight discrepancies. Trim away at the corners so that the lines meet and run around the angle. Lastly, round off the vertical line of the corner and cut into all the mortar lines so that the bricks form 'teeth'. This really gives a solid and believable feel to your walls.

Lightly sanding the floor.

It is generally best to apply primer and any texturing to the brick facia before attaching it to the foam board walls. This is because the brick sheet can warp. Sometimes, if it has been glued to the foam board before this stage, the warping of the brick may force the foam board into a warped shape too. If the priming and texturing is done beforehand, once the brick is dry it can be gently teased back into a flat sheet. It can then be attached to the foam board using UHU® as a contact adhesive along with some pieces of double-sided tape.

Apply the UHU® in several lines, allowing some space for it to spread out. This is particularly important along the outer edges. You want to avoid too much excess glue seeping out. Apply the glue to both surfaces, spreading it out using a small strip of card as a spreader. When you bring the two surfaces together, press them hard together. If some of the brick sheet wants to pull away, use some heavy books to flatten it out until the glue goes off. You can even pin the brick sheet in place if it doesn't matter if the pin goes through the other side.

Once the brick is firmly stuck in place, you can apply a base colour and washes. You could add the colour after the priming and before you stick the sheet to the foam board. However you will most likely need to touch up the corners so that there is a continuity of tone and colour.

For this project you are not creating a naturalistic brick colour but using silver aerosol spray to striking effect. Give the brick a light blast of spray paint. Angle the can so that the spray paint hits the brick sheeting from a sideways direction. This will bring out the brick texture. Because the paint is metallic, the play of light against the wall will be very effective. For a naturalistic effect, you can combine the use of different types of paints, including spray paints, to build up many layers and tones. Try spraying the brick with a light base colour that will get into the mortar lines. Then dry brush some warm tones of reds and ochres over the surface of the brick. When this is dry add some stippling effects in contrasting colours to create highlights and lowlights.

Knock these back with washes and don't be frightened to partially wipe some of the work away with a tissue. Try smearing and smudging some of the colours together, then working back over them with more dry brushing and stippling. Depending how you applied the primer, other textures will start to emerge. For this project start simply. Use white acrylic paint as a primer. Spread it evenly over the whole surface of the brick, then apply a light stippling action. When it is dry, apply the silver spray paint. Just these two simple methods will produce a beautiful and believable textured surface. Now that all your walls are complete, it is time to set them off against a beautifully simple planked, wooden floor.

As with creating the brick wall it is essential to begin with an accurate foundation. Measure out the spacing of the boards and draw them out using your try square and metal rule. Constantly check that the lines are exactly equal and parallel. Use mount board as a base for the floor. If you want to laminate this to a foam base later, you can do so.

When you have marked out the mount board, choose the wood or combination of woods that you would like to make the floor out of. Obeche is the best for a light wood. It will take colour and light washes very well and also looks good in its natural state.

PROJECT: A HUMAN FIGURE IN 1:25 SCALE

Setting the walls off with a planked floor.

Use 1mm thick strips and back them with double-sided tape. Mark out the widths of the planking and cut them out using long, deliberate strokes. As always, score a line first then complete the cut with a second stroke. The strips of obeche that you can buy are quite long. It is more manageable to cut them to size so that they are slightly longer than the whole surface of the floor, or the length of several planks.

Having cut your planks, mix them up so that when you come to stick them to the mount board base, there will be contrasting grain patterns side by side. When you have covered the whole surface with planking, lightly sand the floor, going in the direction of the planks and grain. This unifies the whole floor but still retains the grain and lines of planking.

Finally, set the walls of your room against the floor. Use UHU® if you have used Kapa board as the base to your walls or PVA if it is ordinary foam board. Apply some small pieces of masking tape to temporarily hold the walls and floor in place or put some heavy books across the angle of the walls to weigh it down and ensure the base of the walls make contact with the floor.

Finishing touches

Add your Chippendale chair and human figure to the scene. Decide where to place the figure in relation to the chair, door and window. Are the doors to the rooms open or closed?

It is during this process, when you bring all the modelled elements together, that everything really starts to come to life. This is where you begin to learn the power of models to communicate, not just information about what something might look like or how big it is, but how a model can convey atmosphere or express a narrative. How many stories can you tell?

FURTHER INFORMATION

SUPPLIERS OF MATERIALS

4D Model Shop
www.modelshop.co.uk
Supply the widest range of model making materials in the UK

Tiranti
www.tiranti.co.uk
For sculpting materials and tools.

Cass Arts
www.cass-arts.co.uk
General art materials suppliers aimed at a student budget

London Graphic Centre
www.londongraphics.co.uk
Large and well established supplier of graphics and art materials in Covent Garden

Cowling and Wilcox
www.cowlingandwilcox.com
Well established supplier of art materials.

FURTHER READING

Jackson, Albert, and Day, David *The Model Maker's Handbook* (Random House, 1981)

Neat, David *Model-Making – Materials and Methods* (The Crowood Press, 2008)

Orton, Keith *Model Making for the Stage* (The Crowood Press, 2004)

Payne Christopher T*he Encyclopaedia of Model Making Techniques* (Diane Publishing Company, 2003)

INDEX

A
accelerator (glue) 20, 38, 48
acrylic paint 17, 18
    as primer 76
aluminium 17
aerosol paint 17
    applying 40-41, 42, 76
architectural model 69

B
base colour 55, 76
bead saw 10
blades 9
brass wire 17
brick effect 72-74, 76
Bristol board 14-15, 42, 69

C
chamfering 36-38
card
    Bristol board 14-15
    mount board 14-15
    click pencil 10-11, 46, 69
circles
    cutting 11, 12, 56
clay 15
colouring 49
colour wash 33, 55, 64, 66, 76
contact adhesive 20, 76
copper wire 61
cube
    constructing 29
curves 11
cutting mat 11
cutting out 35, 36, 46

D
display mount 23-24, 43
doors 70
double-sided tape 23, 73
dry brushing 12, 18, 55, 76

F
facia 29
fan brush 12, 33
files 13, 49
flat brush 12
flexible curve 11, 12
foam board 14, 69

G
gesso 18
glue
    aerosol 18, 21-22
    Super Glue 16, 19, 20
    PVA 19
    UHU 19, 20, 73
    wood glue 19
gouache 17, 18

H
hacksaw 9
human figure 61-65

I
ink 18

J
jig 9

K
Kapa board 15

L
laminating 23

M
marking out 35, 51
masking tape 20, 22-23, 31
matchsticks 16
measuring 69
metal
    mesh 17
    rod 17
    rule 10, 27
    sheets 17
    square 10
    wire 17
metallic effect 35, 39, 40
mini file 49
mount board 14, 19, 20, 23

P
paint
    brushes 12-13
    effects 12-13, 18
    variety 17
panelling 69-70
pencil 11
piano wire
planked floor 14, 23, 75-76
Plasticine 15-16, 49, 63
plastics 15
plastic weld 71
pliers 10
postcard 14
primer 18, 32
    spray 40
priming 18, 54, 64, 71

PVA 16, 19
    applying 19, 31

R
rod 17
round-nosed brush 12, 33
ruler
    metal 10
    scale 25

S
sanding 13, 31, 38
sand paper 13
saws 9
scale 25, 45, 61
    rule 25, 60
scalpel
    blade 9
    handle 9
scoring 35, 57-58
sculptural materials
    Milliput 16, 49
    Plasticine 15-16, 49
    Super Sculpey 16
sheet materials 15
soft brush 55
spot gluing 31
spraying 40-41
spray mount 21, 43
stain removal 71
Stanley knife 9
stencil paper 14
sticky-backed product 39
stiff brush 12, 55
stipple brush 13, 32
stippling 47
straight edge 9-11
strengthening 21, 48, 52
string 53
styrene 71
Super Glue 16, 19, 20, 48
Swann-Morton scalpel 9

T
tape
    coloured 23
    double-sided 23
    LX 23
    masking 22-23
    Sellotape 22
texture 32, 35, 41
tissue paper 53, 55
tools 9-11
tracing paper 35, 45
trimming edges 30
try square 10, 29, 30, 59, 69
tweezers 48

U
UHU 19, 20, 73, 76

V
varnish 18, 19

W
water-soluble pencil 55, 56
windows 69
wire
    brass 17
    copper 17, 54, 61
    cutters 17
    fuse 54
    piano 17
    using 53, 54, 61
wood
    balsa 16
    obeche 16, 76
    walnut 16-17
wood stain 18-19, 49

Z
Zip Kicker 21